P9-EDN-955

CULTURES OF THE WORLD
Barbados

Marie Louise Elias and Josie Elias

mc Marshall Cavendish
Benchmark
New York

PICTURE CREDITS

Cover: © Greg Johnston/Danita Delimont
Adina Tovy Amsel/ Lonely Planet Images: 1, 90 • Audrius Tomonis: 135 • David G. Houser: 69, 119, 120, 126 •
Dea/S. Amantini/Getty Images: 37 • Emmanuel Dunand/AFP/Getty Images: 109 • Fox Photos/ Hulton Archive/
Getty Images: 21 • Holger Leue/ Lonely Planet Images: 5, 41, 93, 116, 117, 128 • Hulton Archive/Stringer/
Getty Images: 29 • Hutchison Library: 10, 44, 46, 47, 52, 53, 74, 75, 115 • Josie Elias/Life File: 7, 8, 9, 11, 12, 13,
15, 17, 18, 20, 27, 28, 32, 33, 42, 43, 48, 49, 50, 51, 66, 79, 81, 82, 83, 87, 89, 96, 104, 105, 106, 110, 112, 124 •
Keystone/Getty Images: 31 • Maremagnum/ Getty Images: 54 • Michael Lawrence/Lonely Planet Images: 16
North Wind Picture Archives: 19, 22 • photolibrary: 25, 26, 30, 34, 56, 58, 61, 62, 64, 65, 67, 68, 72, 76, 78, 80,
84, 85, 86, 91, 98, 101, 102, 108, 114, 122, 123, 125, 130, 131 • Richard Cummins/ Lonely Planet Images: 2, 6,
40 • Richard I'Anson/Lonely Planet Images: 55 • Rodrigo Arangua/AFP/Getty Images: 38 • Thony Belizaire/
AFP/Getty Images: 39 • Topham Picturepoint: 23, 35, 45, 111 • Trip Photolibrary: 71, 73, 99, 113, 118 • Yuri
Cortez/ AFP/Getty Images: 36

PRECEDING PAGE
A Barbadian man weaves a basket.

Publisher (U.S.): Michelle Bisson
Editors: Deborah Grahame, Stephanie Pee
Copyreader: Sherry Chiger
Designers: Nancy Sabato, Benson Tan
Cover picture researcher: Connie Gardner
Picture researcher: Thomas Khoo

Marshall Cavendish Benchmark
99 White Plains Road
Tarrytown, NY 10591
Website: www.marshallcavendish.us

Library of Congress Cataloging-in-Publication Data
Elias, Marie Louise.
  Barbados / by Marie Louise Elias and Josie Elias. — 2nd ed.
    p. cm. — (Cultures of the world)
  Summary: "Provides comprehensive information on the geography, history, wildlife, governmental
structure, economy, cultural diversity, peoples, religion, and culture of Barbados"—Provided by publisher.
  Includes bibliographical references and index.
  ISBN 978-0-7614-4853-2
  1. Barbados—Juvenile literature. I. Elias, Josie. II. Title.
  F2041.E45 2010
  972.981--dc22   2009044592

Printed in China
9 8 7 6 5 4 3 2 1

CONTENTS

INTRODUCTION

A **SMALL ISLAND NATION WITH AN ESTIMATED POPULATION OF** 284,589 people, Barbados is part of the Lesser Antilles of the Caribbean. It is an island of great natural beauty with two distinct coastlines—the dramatic eastern coast with cliffs braced against thundering Atlantic breakers and the white sandy beaches and gentle waters of the west.

Barbadians are well educated, with a 99.7 percent literacy rate. The government has invested in education and training as a means of developing Barbados's main resource—its people. From an economy based on sugar, Barbados is moving toward a services-orientated economy where tourism is the main revenue earner.

Barbados is the result of more than 300 years of British heritage. The institution of slavery has also been a factor in the shaping of Barbadian culture. Political stability, a congenial climate, and a relaxed and fun-loving population combine to make Barbados one of the most attractive tourist destinations in the West Indies.

This book examines this enchanting island surrounded by coral reefs and provides an insight into what makes Barbados's multiracial society so appealing to the rest of the world.

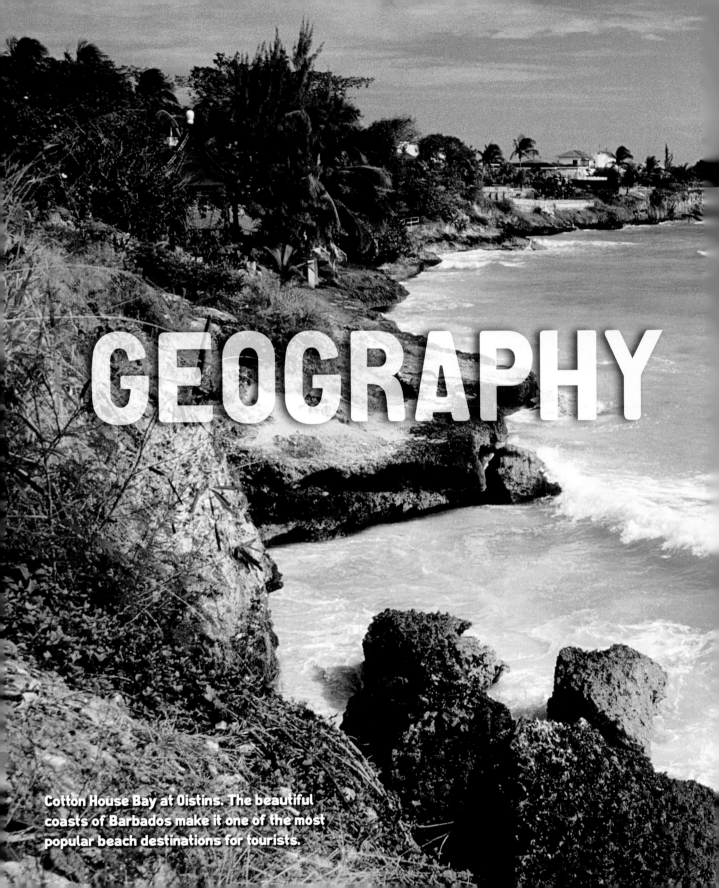

GEOGRAPHY

Cotton House Bay at Oistins. The beautiful coasts of Barbados make it one of the most popular beach destinations for tourists.

CHAPTER 1

BARBADOS IS A PEAR-SHAPE ISLAND, 21 miles (34 km) long and 14 miles (23 km) across at its widest, with a total land area of 166 square miles (431 square km). Approximately 300 miles (483 km) north of Venezuela and 100 miles (161 km) east of the Caribbean chain, Barbados lies at 13°10"N, 59°32"W, the most easterly island of the West Indies.

TOPOGRAPHY

Geologically Barbados is a relatively young island—it is only about a million years old. Unlike its neighbors to the west, which were formed

The rugged coastline at North Point in the parish of Saint Lucy.

With 60 miles (97 km) of coastline, the island of Barbados is about three times the size of Washington, D.C., and is the easternmost Caribbean island in the northern Atlantic Ocean. It has a tropical climate with a rainy season (June to October) and is relatively flat, rising to a central highland region, with the highest point, Mount Hillaby, at 1,125 feet (343 m) above sea level.

The jagged hilltops of Chalky Mount in Saint Andrew's Parish consist of rocks striped in hues of pink, gray, and ocher, twisted and folded almost vertically during geological upheavals.

Hackleton's Cliff in the east towers 1,000 feet (305 m) over the coast and is several miles long. It was formed when the eastern side of the island rose and tilted gently to the west. Waves pounding at the base of the cliff and raging waterfalls dislodged enormous boulders, which tumbled to the sea at Bathsheba.

by volcanic activity, it is composed of coral limestone accumulations on a ridge of submarine debris on the seabed, which collected sand and grit from the Orinoco River in South America.

Tectonic forces pushed the coral out of the water, forming two small islands. Today's central plateau around Mount Hillaby was once divided from the southern ridge of Christ Church by a shallow sea covering what is now Saint George Valley. The landmass, covered by a cap of coral stone, tilted as it rose, forming high cliffs to the east and a series of ridges and terraces to the west. Water permeating the island's porous limestone created underground streams, springs, and caverns. Surrounded by coral reefs, most of the island is relatively flat.

The west coast, with its white sandy beaches and calm blue waters, has become the center of Barbados's tourist industry. Most of the island's resorts and hotels are located there or in the south. In contrast, high waves beat against the rocks and rugged cliffs of the less developed east coast. The north is the least populated region.

In the relatively hilly northeast, known as the Scotland District, erosion has removed much of the thick coral cover found on the rest of the island. Barbados's highest point, Mount Hillaby, rises to 1,125 feet (343 m) in the north-central part of the island.

The island is divided into 11 parishes, or local administrative units, a legacy of the clergy's powerful influence in the past.

CLIMATE

Barbados has a tropical climate. Temperatures in January range from 75°F (24°C) to 84°F (29°C), and in July they increase only by a couple of degrees. The driest months are February to June, with a mean humidity of 68 percent. The rest of the year the humidity averages between 74 percent and 79 percent. July is the wettest month, and annual rainfall averages 45 inches (114 cm).

HURRICANES The hurricane season in the Caribbean is from June to October, with hurricanes occurring most frequently in August and September. This region has one of the world's highest rates of hurricanes per year. Major hurricanes hit Barbados in 1667, 1731, 1780, 1831, and 1955, causing loss of life and extensive damage to property, but usually the storms bypass the island to the north.

Hurricanes originate when high winds revolve in a counterclockwise direction around a center of lower barometric pressure. When the winds stay

Many of the larger churches around the island have the words "hurricane shelter" painted either on a wall or on their gates.

below 40 miles per hour (64 km per hour), it is known as a tropical depression. Winds between 40 and 75 miles per hour (64 and 121 km per hour) become a tropical storm. Only winds of at least 75 miles per hour (121 km per hour) qualify as hurricanes.

VEGETATION

Seeds of mangroves, sea coconuts, sea grapes, sea spurges, sea beans, French cotton, and manchineels probably drifted to Barbados from South America hundreds of thousands of years ago. Once established, these plants stabilized the coastline. Coconuts, horse nicker, and lavender floated from Africa, while wind-borne seeds came with Sahara dust. Gradually a forest developed. Most of the native forests were cleared by early settlers for farming. The landscape now consists predominantly of sugarcane fields, pastures, and scrubland. The remaining woodlands are mainly found where gullies and cliffs make the land unsuitable for agriculture.

Rich agricultural land in Saint George Valley in the south of Barbados.

THE BAOBAB

The baobab tree (Adansonia digitata), also known as the monkey-bread tree, is said to have been brought to Barbados around 1738 from Africa. It takes 15 adults joined with outstretched arms to encircle one such tree in Queen's Park in Bridgetown.

Only a few areas, such as Grenade Hall Forest, have remained comparatively untouched. Turner's Hall Wood in the parish of Saint Andrew is a remnant of the dense tropical forest that covered the island at the time of the first settlement. Fine examples of silk cotton, sandbox tree, trumpet tree, cabbage palm, and the indigenous macaw palm grow there. Other trees common to Barbados include the giant bearded fig (*Ficus citrofolia*), casuarina, white cedar, poinciana, locust, and mahogany.

Welchman Hall Gully, a deep ravine planted in the 1860s, is well known for its groves of citrus and spice-bearing trees as well as many rare trees.

ANIMAL LIFE

A few introduced species of mammals such as mongooses, vervet monkeys (*Cercopithecus aethiops*), hares, mice, and rats can be found in the wild. A nonpoisonous and rarely seen grass snake known as the Barbados racer (*Liophis perfuscus*) is found only on Barbados, but there are other harmless blind snakes, whistling frogs, lizards, red-footed tortoises, and eight species

A red-footed tortoise in Saint Peter.

GREEN MONKEYS

Introduced as pets from West Africa some 350 years ago, vervet, or green, monkeys quickly found their way into the wild, where with no predators, they multiplied rapidly. Because monkeys have the same food preferences as humans, they have always been considered pests by farmers, who can lose up to a third of their banana, mango, and papaya crops to them.

Today the island's monkey population is estimated at between 5,000 and 10,000. As they are neither rare nor endangered, either on the island or worldwide, the government has long encouraged the hunting of monkeys. The first bounties were introduced as early as the late 1600s, but in 1975 the Ministry of Agriculture introduced a bounty of Bds$5 for every monkey tail. After the Barbados Primate Research Center was founded in 1980, a more enticing reward of Bds$50 was offered for each monkey captured alive and delivered unharmed to the center. As a result, monkeys are now usually trapped rather than shot.

of bats. Hawksbill turtles lay their eggs on the sandy beaches, and the leatherback turtle is an occasional nester.

Although more than 180 species of birds have been sighted on Barbados, most are migrating shorebirds and waders that stop over from North America on their way to winter feeding grounds in South America. Only 28 species actually nest on Barbados, including wood doves, blackbirds, banana quits, guinea fowl, cattle egrets, herons, finches, and three kinds of hummingbirds.

The seas around Barbados abound with more than 50 varieties of fish, providing a source of livelihood for many people. Surface-dwelling fish of the open seas (pelagic fish) are found 5 to 25 miles (8 to 40 km) offshore. Dolphins, kingfish, billfish, sharks, flying fish, and bonitos fall into this category. Big game fish include blue marlin—one weighing 911 pounds (413 kg) was caught off Barbados in 1996—white marlin, sailfish, and tuna. Coral reefs are home to a rich marine life, including ning-nings, lobsters, moray eels, octopuses, and gorgonias.

MAIN TOWNS

BRIDGETOWN in the parish of Saint Michael is the island's capital and commercial center. It has a population of about 80,000 and was founded in 1628 on Carlisle Bay, the island's only natural harbor.

Bridgetown's main street includes some restored colonial buildings. The Careenage, an inlet now lined with recreational boats, cuts into the heart of the city. Interisland schooners carrying fresh produce and other goods docked here for 300 years, while sailing ships sought harbor in the outer basin or were careened (turned sideways so that their hull could be scraped and cleaned) in the inner basin. Before the construction of Bridgetown Harbor in 1961, large vessels and dreadnoughts anchored in Carlisle Bay.

Independence Arch, which commemorates Bajan, or Barbadian, independence, is at the south side of Chamberlain Bridge, which crosses the Careenage to Trafalgar Square. This square marks the bustling center of the city's political, financial, commercial, and seafaring life. On Remembrance Day, military parades fill the square, and poppy wreaths are laid at the Cenotaph, an obelisk monument erected in 1925 to honor those killed in World War I.

HOLETOWN is in the sophisticated parish of Saint James. It was originally called Jamestown by the first English settlers, who landed here in 1627 aboard the *Olive Blossom* and claimed the island in the name of King James I of England. An obelisk monument and a mural running along the main road in the town center commemorate this event, but the date on the monument, July 1605, is two decades early. A recent development has incorporated the monument, the post office, and the police station into a compound reminiscent of those early days.

Speightstown is the main town in the north.

SPEIGHTSTOWN, in the parish of Saint Peter, was named after a 1639 member of Parliament, William Speight. It was once dubbed Little Bristol because it was the main shipping line to Bristol, England, when sugar was Barbados's mainstay. A quiet place, slightly off the beaten track, it is the only town on the island to retain many of its original small streets lined with simple two-story houses, some of which have Georgian-style balconies and overhanging galleries.

OISTINS, in the parish of Christ Church, is the center of the island's fishing industry. It has a large and bustling fish market open daily as long as the catch—dolphin, shark, barracuda, snapper, and flying fish—keeps arriving. The government has built a Bds$10 million fisheries terminal to encourage modernization of the fishing industry. The growing number of deep-sea fishing boats, which have replaced smaller vessels, make good use of the new ice machines in the terminal.

HISTORY

An old stone sugar mill. Sugar production was an important part of Barbados's past, and continues to be essential to its economy today.

UNLIKE SOME OF ITS CARIBBEAN neighbors, Barbados was never visited by Christopher Columbus, the renowned Italian explorer in the service of Spanish monarchs Ferdinand II of Aragon and Isabella I of Castile, who had united several kingdoms of the Iberian Peninsula by marrying and ruling together.

Although the name *Los Barbados* is is mentioned in Spanish cedulas (formal official orders) in 1511 and 1512, Columbus passed it by in favor of the larger islands nearby. The first Europeans to note the island on their maps were the Portuguese, but it was not until early in the 17th century that Barbados was claimed by English explorers.

Old cannons in the Garrison in Bridgetown.

Barbados acquired the nickname "Little England" because it is the most British of the Caribbean islands. It was not conquered and reconquered many times, as were some of the other Caribbean islands, because winds and currents made it relatively difficult to reach by sail. British control lasted from 1625 until independence in 1966.

THE FIRST BARBADIANS

The history of the early settlement of Barbados is being reconsidered because of recent archaeological discoveries. Artifacts and other evidence unearthed at Port Saint Charles point to a first settlement around 1623 B.C. Among the items unearthed were several stacks of pots that turned out to be a very primitive form of water well. This is thought to be the largest collection of stacks of pots ever found in the West Indies and Central America and is being studied by archaeologists, but very little is known about the people who inhabited the settlement. However, this settlement certainly predates the Saladoid-Barrancoid Amerindians who came from Venezuela and were previously thought to be the earliest permanent settlers.

A subsequent movement of Amerindian migrants known as the Arawaks arrived around A.D. 800. The Arawaks were skilled farmers and fishermen and accomplished in the ceramic crafts, which they traded among other communities throughout the Caribbean area. They were short, olive-skinned, and handsome. Their villages, sited in sheltered freshwater bays, were strung along the coastline in areas where the fishing grounds were good, particularly at the northeastern tip of the island. The Arawaks cultivated cassava, potatoes, and corn. They made *casareep* (ka-sa-REEP) from grated or ground cassava, a unique flavoring still used in Caribbean cuisine today.

These early settlers lived harmoniously in relative isolation in Barbados until about 1250, when the Caribs, a taller, stronger tribe, arrived. The Caribs

Barbados may have been named after the bearded fig trees found on the island.

were a warlike and savage group. The Spanish named this tribe *Caribes*, which means "cannibals" and which gave the region its name, Caribbean. In fact, the Caribs did practice cannibalism, but human flesh was not eaten as food; it was used in rituals to gain control over the dead enemies or to acquire the qualities of dead ancestors.

The Amerindians' existence was disrupted in 1492 when the Spanish conquistadores began raiding the island for slaves to work in the sugar estates and mines in Hispaniola. The raiders also brought with them European diseases to which the Amerindians had little or no resistance. Those who did not get sick and managed to evade the slave raids escaped to the neighboring Windward Islands, where they could consolidate their defenses against the Spaniards. Barbados was effectively abandoned by its early Native American settlers because the island's lack of mountains made it difficult for them to defend themselves from raiders.

In 1536 Portuguese explorer Pedro a Campos, on his way to Brazil, claimed that the island was uninhabited. He is said to have given the island its name of Los Barbados (the Bearded Ones), presumably after the fig trees with long-hanging aerial roots that have a beardlike appearance. Barbados's name is thus Portuguese in origin.

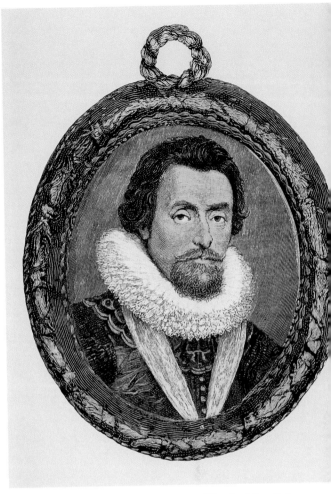

The first English settlement on Barbados was named for King James I, who ruled from 1603 to 1625.

ARRIVAL OF THE ENGLISH

When Captain John Powell landed on Barbados in May 1625 and claimed it for King James I of England, all he found was a flourishing herd of wild hogs, descendants of those left behind by the Portuguese. The first English settlement was established in Jamestown (now Holetown) in February 1627

Dripstones made of coral limestone were once used to filter drinking water taken from wells, ponds, or springs before piped water provided a more reliable supply.

when Captain Henry Powell landed with a party of 80 settlers and 10 black slaves.

Financed by merchant Sir William Courteen and associates, the pioneer colonists were employees rather than freehold farmers. They owned neither land nor stock. Helped by white indentured servants and meeting no armed resistance, these settlers were able to concentrate on the immediate task of planting crops and establishing trade systems. Because other English settlements in the West Indies were hampered by continuous native opposition, Barbados quickly surpassed them all, both in population growth and in commercial activity.

THE CREATION OF PLANTOCRACY

In 1639 Governor Henry Hawley established the House of Assembly. The land tenure system was changed, and lands were issued to colonists in return for a quitrent of 40 pounds (18 kg) of tobacco annually. Only men with large sums of capital could afford to become substantial landholders, so a society dominated by a small, landed elite developed. Lands were effectively allocated to colonists with known financial and social connections in England. English law and tradition took hold quickly, and the island became known as "Little England."

THE FIRST CROPS Barbados was described as a colony "built on smoke" because at first tobacco was its only export. By 1631, however, planters were cultivating cotton, which was fetching high prices in London. Boom conditions prevailed until 1639, when the London market was oversupplied with cotton. Prices fell sharply, and the colonists had to find a new crop.

INDENTURED SERVANTS The production of tobacco, cotton, and indigo relied heavily on a labor force of British indentured servants. More than half of the whites who came to Barbados during the 1630s and '40s were indentured servants, contracted to serve their employers for five years (if over 21 years old) or up to seven years (if under 21) in return for passage to the colony and subsistence on arrival.

Indentured servants were little more than slaves. They could be bought or sold, even gambled away. They were not permitted to leave their plantations without a pass signed by their master. Their contracts gave them certain rights, such as the receipt of adequate food, clothing, and shelter and the right to complain to local magistrates of mistreatment by their masters.

Because planters believed they could treat their "property" in whatever way they wished within the limits of the "customs of the country," these rights were seldom exercised. The descendants of these Scottish, Irish, and Welsh indentured servants would later be known as "red legs," the name coming from the sunburned skin on their kilt-exposed legs.

Workers on a sugarcane plantation in Barbados.

INTRODUCTION OF SUGARCANE

Sugarcane was brought to the island in 1637 by a Dutchman who had learned how to grow and process it in Brazil. Defeated by the Portuguese in Brazil, the Dutch needed a market for their sugar-making machinery and their slave trade. Dutch merchants therefore helped struggling English colonists grow

A woodcut of a slave ship.

sugarcane so that these farmers would then need to purchase slaves to cultivate the crop and machinery to process it.

By 1645 Barbados was flourishing. Five years later it was described as the richest spot in the New World. Barbadians dominated the sugar industry in the early years as the wealth of the planter class increased. Large sugarcane estates were formed by combining smaller ones that did not have access to sufficient capital.

During the next 15 years the number of landholders declined substantially. Although they made up fewer than 10 percent of the island's population, the elite plantocracy dominated public life and civic organizations and made sure that only white, Anglo-Saxon Anglicans were allowed any political or legal power. Some of them received knighthoods or baronetcies in the second half of the century.

CHARTER OF BARBADOS

The English Parliament, after the execution of King Charles I in 1649, decided planters in Barbados were rebels and launched an operation to subdue the colony. A fleet under Sir George Ayscue blockaded the island until early 1652, when the colonists accepted the terms offered by Ayscue's delegation and signed articles of capitulation, agreeing to recognize the rule of Parliament and the colony's governor in return for continued self-government, free trade, and the restoration of confiscated properties.

This formed the basis for the Charter of Barbados, which guaranteed government by a governor and a freely elected assembly as well as freedom from taxation without local consent. When the monarchy was restored in England in 1660, this charter provided Barbados with a greater measure of independence from the monarchy than any of the other British colonies.

INTRODUCTION OF SLAVES

Large numbers of slaves had to be brought in to work in the sugar fields, mills, boiling houses, and distilleries. The plantations could not have existed without these slaves, who came to Barbados from West Africa. They were of many ethnic groups, speaking different languages.

The field slaves were housed in floorless huts, given meager food, and forced to work 12 hours a day, six days a week. Skilled slaves such as carpenters, blacksmiths, and tailors fared better, and domestic slaves were more trusted and better treated than field workers.

A sketch of slaves harvesting sugarcane.

FIRST SLAVE ACTS During the sugar boom, the slave population rose from 5,680 in 1645 to 60,000 by 1684, at which point the slaves outnumbered the whites by three to one. Acts were passed to control this vast labor force. The 1688 act declared slaves to be "real estate," which legally tied them to specific plantations and meant that they could neither own property nor give evidence in court against whites. In addition, slaves could not leave their plantation without a ticket signed by their master, and they were forbidden to beat drums, blow horns, or use other loud instruments.

ABORTED SLAVE REBELLIONS From the very beginning, Africans resisted their enslavement in Barbados. Plantation houses were built to incorporate defenses against slave attacks. The first recorded incident was a small-scale uprising in 1649. In 1675, however, a planned revolt by African-born slaves involving a large number of plantations across the island was discovered, and the ringleaders were arrested and executed.

A more widespread conspiracy, which involved plans for slaves to form themselves into four regiments of foot soldiers and two mounted regiments with the intention of bringing the entire island under black control, was exposed in 1692. Of the 200 to 300 slaves who were arrested and brought to trial, 92 were executed.

No attempted rebellions were recorded in Barbados between 1702 and 1815, partly because the white community established and maintained a powerful island-wide system for the control of slaves, with dozens of forts strung along the coast. Slaves did run away, but they could not form large runaway communities as slaves on some of the larger Caribbean islands did, because there was nowhere safe to establish them. Recent historical research has shown that there was a high level of slave resistance, but even so there was only a single actual outbreak of armed revolt, which became known as the Bussa Rebellion or the Rebellion of 1816.

THE 18TH CENTURY

Barbados languished during the 18th century. Trade competition from islands such as Jamaica and Saint Kitts intensified, and the price of sugar fell sharply. Britain was at war with France in the Americas, and that combined with the American War of Independence caused trade between Barbados and the British colonies in America to plummet, cutting off food supplies and material for the sugar industry. Food shortages became so serious that the poor died in the streets.

Barbados also suffered several other calamities. Yellow fever in 1703 caused many deaths. A hurricane in 1731 wreaked widespread damage and was followed by a drought two years later. An even more destructive hurricane struck in 1780, destroying crops and killing nearly 22,000 people in Barbados, Saint Lucia, Saint Vincent, and Martinique, with about 4,500 dead in Barbados alone.

Gun Hill Signal Station was an important military post that was used to alert troops in the event of an invasion.

Recognizing Barbados's strategic location, the English used the colony as part of a multi-island defense center. British regiments were stationed in imposing arched brick buildings in the garrison in Bridgetown. By 1795, Barbados had 22 forts, 450 guns, and a series of elevated signal stations that could relay signals to alert the entire island within minutes of a sighting of an aggressor to the north or the south. The victory of Vice Admiral Horatio Nelson at Trafalgar, Spain, in 1805 and the military success of English troops in the West Indies stabilized sugar markets.

THE END OF SLAVERY

The abolition of the slave trade in 1807 caused the plantocracy little concern, even though Barbadian blacks had become more aggressive after Haitian revolutionaries had declared independence in 1804. This was especially true of the artisan and domestic slaves, who were better informed than the field workers and considered themselves closer to freedom.

Lord Nelson's crucial victory over the combined French and Spanish fleets at the Battle of Trafalgar not only saved Britain from invasion, but it also ensured the supremacy of British sea power for another century.

The Emancipation Act was passed into law in 1833 and took effect on August 1, 1834. All slaves under the age of six were unconditionally emancipated. Slaves over the age of six were freed but had to continue to serve their former owners as unpaid apprentices for six years. This was intended to give the slaves time to adjust gradually to freedom and the slave owners the opportunity to reorganize their plantations around wage laborers.

Instead of improving working conditions for the former slaves, the act had the opposite effect. The planters' attitude to their workforce hardened, and workers became sullen and unproductive. When the planters abandoned all responsibility for infants, workers had to struggle to provide for their children, and many of the 14,000 children who had been freed in 1834 joined the ranks of the destitute in the colony. It soon became clear that the apprenticeship system was a farce, and on August 1, 1838, all slaves were fully emancipated, two years ahead of schedule.

An illustration of former slaves celebrating their emancipation.

THE TWENTIETH CENTURY

Subsidized sugar beet production in Europe caused a crisis for Barbados's sugar industry during the mid-1890s, and many indebted estates were sold to the urban merchant class. Thus bolstered by the wealth of the merchant families, the plantocracy entered the 20th century secure in their ability to rule in the difficult times ahead.

HORATIO LORD NELSON

The bronze statue of Horatio Nelson, who sailed into Barbados in 1805 a few months before dying at the Battle of Trafalgar, was erected in Bridgetown in 1813, two decades before its larger London counterpart. Over the years the statue has been the subject of controversy among the islanders, some of whom feel it embraces the island's colonial past too closely. In the 1970s the Mighty Gabby, a leading calypso singer, had a popular song called "Take Down Nelson" that suggested replacing Nelson with a Bajan man.

The British government's growing concern for the welfare of the working class found little support among the Barbadian planters, who remained determined to keep their plantation labor in line and restrict the education of black children to discourage them from seeking employment outside agriculture. Although ownership of their own piece of land was the ambition of nearly every plantation worker, very few succeeded in obtaining freehold.

PANAMA MAN The resumption of construction on the Panama Canal by the United States in 1904 provided male Barbadian workers with an opportunity to escape from plantation work. Planters subsequently employed women to do "men's work" at lower wages.

Some 20,000 men emigrated to Panama. Former field hands returning from Panama had enough money to buy land, open shops, learn a craft, or acquire education for clerical or business professions. A slump in sugar prices forced indebted planters to sell some of their plantations in small lots to these "Panama men," and the pattern of landownership changed significantly.

Commemorated by the Emancipation Statue, which was unveiled in 1985 at the border between Saint Michael and Saint George parishes, the Bussa Rebellion was the result of a misunderstanding. In 1815 Britain passed a bill declaring that all slaves in the West Indies had to be registered. Believing this bill was a threat to their right of self-government, the Barbadian House of Assembly rejected it. The slaves thought the bill was not to register them but intended to free them. It was the unfulfilled expectation of freedom that sparked the rebellion.

An African-born slave called Bussa was the primary leader. Rebel contingents assembled at his plantation in Saint Philip, where sugarcane fields were set alight. The revolt spread but was eventually suppressed by the British militia. Bussa is believed to have died in battle as the head of his contingent during the final showdown.

Although many of the workers returning from Panama were able to achieve a better quality of life, for the majority of the working class, conditions deteriorated.

BLACK POWER Education, societies for the working class, and the Barbados Labor Union (formed in 1919) provided the background for the development of a radical political movement in Barbados, abetted by Marcus Garvey's pan-Caribbean and international "black power" movement.

Grantley Adams was the founder of the Barbados Labor Party.

During the 1930s the combination of a rapidly growing population, the rising cost of living, and dissatisfaction with wages fixed at the equivalent of 30 cents a day sparked street riots in Barbados. Fourteen people were killed and 47 were wounded in protests in 1937. The rioting spurred Grantley Adams to found the Barbados Labor Party (BLP) in 1938. During the 1942 House of Assembly session, Adams led a fight for reforms that allowed more people to qualify to vote, increased direct taxation, and established a workers' compensation program. Adams became the island's first premier in 1954 and was knighted in 1957.

INDEPENDENCE Errol Walton Barrow was a fervent social reformer who replaced Sir Grantley Adams as premier in 1961 when the Democratic Labor Party (DLP) gained power as a liberal alternative to the conservative BLP. Barbados was able to function autonomously through a peaceful democratic process, and this resulted in the negotiation of its independence at a constitutional conference with the United Kingdom in 1966, at which point it became an independent nation within the commonwealth.

GOVERNMENT

Clocktower of the Parliament House in Bridgetown.

U NIQUE AMONG THE ISLANDS OF the Caribbean, Barbados was ruled by Britain for an unbroken stretch of more than 300 years. Today it maintains strong links with Britain. This has helped to create a foundation of stability in a country made up of different races and creeds.

THE CONSTITUTION

Barbados's political system is a constitutional monarchy, with Queen Elizabeth II as head of state, represented by the governor-general,

Barbados welcomes Queen Elizabeth II during an official visit in 1966.

Barbados is governed by a system of constitutional monarchy and parliamentary government with democratic traditions. The island is divided into 30 constituencies. The people of Barbados enjoy many constitutional safeguards, including freedom of speech, worship, press, movement, and association.

Independent Arch in Bridgetown commemorates the country's gaining of independence on November 30, 1966.

Sir Clifford Husbands. The constitution dates from 1966 and provides for a system of parliamentary government on the British model, with a prime minister and cabinet drawn from and responsible to the legislature, which consists of a Senate and a House of Assembly.

THE SENATE AND THE HOUSE OF ASSEMBLY

The Senate consists of 21 members appointed by the governor-general: 12 on the advice of the prime minister, two on the advice of the leader of the opposition, and the rest on the basis of wider consultations. The House of Assembly, which dates back to 1639, has 28 members elected by adult suffrage. The voting age is 18 years.

The Parliament House in Bridgetown is the seat of Barbados's Senate and House of Assembly.

Each legislature has a maximum tenure of five years and can be dissolved anytime during this period. The governor-general appoints both the prime minister—on the basis of support in the House of Assembly—and the leader of the opposition. Cabinet ministers are also appointed by the governor-general, on the advice of the prime minister.

POLITICAL PARTIES AND MAJOR POLITICIANS

THE BARBADOS LABOR PARTY (moderate left of center) won the first general election in 1951. It was formed in 1938 by Grantley Adams, who became premier in 1954 when ministerial government was established.

A statue of Grantley Adams.

SIR GRANTLEY ADAMS A lawyer who had won the Barbados Scholarship to Oxford University in 1918, Sir Grantley Adams became the most important figure in preindependence politics. He rose to prominence through his testimony before Britain's Moyne Commission investigating regional disturbances in the late 1930s, claiming that the riots were caused mainly by economic distress.

Elected to the House of Assembly in 1940 and president-general of the Barbados Workers' Union in 1941, he became leader of the government in 1946. In 1951, in the first election conducted under universal adult suffrage with no property qualifications, the BLP won 16 of the 24 seats, thus gaining a majority. Adams was knighted in 1952. He is the only person ever to hold the office of prime minister of the West Indies Federation, which was dissolved in 1962 when Jamaica and Trinidad and Tobago opted for independence.

Under his leadership, Barbados was transformed from an oligarchy into a democracy based on universal suffrage. A wide range of social reforms were introduced, and major construction projects such as Bridgetown's Deep Water Harbor were started.

THE DEMOCRATIC LABOR PARTY (moderate left of center) was formed in 1955. When full internal self-government was achieved in 1961, the party won the general election under leader Errol Barrow, who became the first prime minister when full independence was gained in 1966.

ERROL BARROW Barrow served in the British Royal Air Force during World War II and subsequently studied law in London. He returned to Barbados in 1950, joined the BLP, and was elected to the House of Assembly in 1951. He became the leader of a discontented BLP left wing, which felt that Adams was too close to the governor and not giving enough attention to the workers.

Errol Barrow was the prime minister of Barbados from 1966 to 1976 and from 1986 to 1987.

In 1954 Barrow left the BLP. The following year he founded the DLP, which he led for the next 32 years. He gained the support of sugar workers demanding higher wages, and his party won the 1961 elections. Between 1961 and 1966, the DLP replaced the legislative council with a senate appointed by the governor, increased workers' benefits, instituted a program for industrialization, and expanded free education.

The sixth prime minister of Barbados, David Thompson was elected in 2008.

The DLP won the November 1966 elections, and Barrow became the country's first prime minister when Barbados gained its independence on November 30, 1966. Significant achievements during his period in office included the introduction of free secondary and university education and the lowering of the voting age to 18.

The BLP was reelected in 1976 under Sir Grantley Adams's son, Tom, who died suddenly in 1985 and was succeeded by Harold Bernard St. John. The following year the DLP, led by Barrow, returned to power with 24 of the 27 seats in the House of Assembly. Barrow died suddenly in 1987 and was succeeded by the deputy prime minister, Lloyd Erskine Sandiford.

A new opposition party, the National Democratic Party (centrist), was formed in 1989 by Richard Haynes, a former minister of finance in Sandiford's cabinet. In 1990 the Electoral and Boundaries Commission increased the number of seats in the House of Assembly from 27 to 30. The DLP, under Sandiford, won the general election in 1991. In 1994 Owen Seymour Arthur became prime minister after leading the BLP to victory in 19 of the 28 seats in the House of Assembly, securing 48 percent of the vote. David Thompson became the sixth prime minister in January 2008 after the DLP won the general election with 20 seats against 10 for the BLP.

NATIONAL SECURITY

During the 17th and 18th centuries, Barbados was an important military base for the British, enabling them to protect their interests in the Caribbean. The many antiquated cannons still found on the island are a reminder of those turbulent times when Barbados held a vital role in regional power.

A military parade in Bridgetown.

Today Barbados is a peaceful island with little crime, and it no longer requires a large military force. The Barbados Defense Force, established in 1978, has a strength of

500	armed forces personnel
110	navy (coast guard)
430	reserve force.

Barbados also has a police force of about 1,400 that includes the Harbour Police and the Corps of Writ Servers.

FOREIGN RELATIONS

Both the DLP and the BLP are committed to maintaining free enterprise and alignment with the United States. In 1972 the DLP government reestablished

The Organization of American States (OAS) was established as the International Union of American Republics at a meeting in Washington, D.C., in 1890. The main objectives of the OAS include strengthening the peace and security of North, Central, and South America; ensuring the peaceful settlement of disputes among member states; and promoting economic, social, and cultural development through cooperative action.

Most countries in North, South, and Central America as well as the Caribbean, including the United States, are members of the OAS. A notable exception, however, is Cuba; its membership has been suspended since 1962. The OAS is headquartered in Washington, D.C., and has an annual budget of about $100 million contributed by member governments. Every member nation has one vote, and unlike in the United Nations, no country has veto power.

diplomatic relations with Cuba while maintaining cordial relations with the United States. In 1979, in a move described by Prime Minister Tom Adams as an act of "East Caribbean defense cooperation," the BLP administration dispatched troops to Saint Vincent to help maintain order when Saint Vincent police were deployed in containing an uprising on the Grenadines' Union Island.

In 1983 the BLP government participated in the U.S. invasion of Grenada. This action, however, strained relations with Trinidad, which claimed that the operation was undertaken without proper consultation of all members of the Caribbean Community (CARICOM).

Barbados's foreign minister, Bertie Miller (*left*), with Haitian prime minister Gerard Latortue (*right*).

Barbados is a member of international organizations including the United Nations (UN), the Organization of American States (OAS), CARICOM, the Commonwealth of Nations, and the Inter-American Development Bank (IDB). In 2008 Barbados and the other members of CARICOM signed an Economic Partnership Agreement (EPA) with the European Union (EU) and its European Commission. This deal covers CARICOM's membership in the Caribbean Forum (CARIFORUM). CARIFORUM is part of the Group of African, Caribbean, and Pacific (ACP) States. The agreement outlines Barbados's trade ties and future development with the EU. Countries with diplomatic representation in Barbados include Brazil, Canada, the People's Republic of China, Colombia, Costa Rica, the United Kingdom, the United States, and Venezuela. Barbados has established official diplomatic relations with 103 countries worldwide.

The Commonwealth of Nations is a free association of 53 independent nations. Most members are former British colonies. Barbados was admitted into the Commonwealth in 1966, when it gained independence.

ECONOMY

A container ship docking at the port in Bridgetown.

CHAPTER 4

T HE ECONOMY OF BARBADOS is based on four main sectors: tourism, offshore financial services, agriculture including fishing, and manufacturing.

TOURISM

The tourist industry had its origins in the years just before World War I, catering to winter visitors from North America and the United Kingdom as well as visitors from Latin America, particularly Brazil. The colony owed its increasing prosperity to such visitors, but the tourist industry remained subordinate to the sugar industry until the 1970s.

Schoolchildren on a field trip to the Barbados Wildlife Reserve at Farley Hill.

The economy of Barbados has changed through the years, with the dominance of the sugarcane industry giving way to the growth of tourism. It shrank briefly after 9/11 and the associated global decline in tourism, but economic growth returned in 2004. The island has to import essential goods, and its economy is therefore a small open economy, meaning that it is unable to influence the prices it must pay to trade with other countries.

AN EARLY TOURIST

In 1751, more than two decades before he became the first president of the United States, George Washington came to Barbados with his half-brother Lawrence, who suffered from tuberculosis and was hoping that the tropical climate would prove therapeutic. Unfortunately George contracted smallpox while on Barbados, which left his face scarred, and Lawrence died the following year. The Barbados trip was the only overseas journey George Washington ever made.

The Central Bank of Barbados was established in 1972.

Tourism is now crucial to the economy, with the service sector as a whole representing approximately 80 percent of gross domestic product (GDP). About 10 percent of the working population—some 13,000 people—are employed in the tourism sector. In 2007 Barbados hosted the World Cricket Cup, which attracted visitors and helped improve growth figures of the construction, communication, utilities, and tourism sectors.

OFFSHORE FINANCIAL SERVICES

Barbados has been actively encouraging international offshore companies such as banks, insurers, trusts, and shipping registration companies to register in the country by exempting them from capital gains tax and estate duty. Tax breaks and incentives make the island an attractive investment opportunity. The government agency responsible for the establishment and expansion of business enterprises is the Barbados Investment and Development Corporation (BIDC).

AGRICULTURE

Although the government has embarked on a policy of agricultural diversification to increase the production of fruits, vegetables, poultry, and

A banana plantation in Saint Joseph. The Barbadian government is taking steps to diversify its agricultural production.

meat, sugarcane is still the main cash crop and makes a large contribution to the island's export earnings.

SUGARCANE (*Saccharum officinarum*) is a giant, thick perennial grass cultivated for its sweet sap. The plant grows in clumps of solid stalks and has graceful, sword-shape leaves. Mature canes can grow from 10 to 26 feet (3 to 8 m) tall and from 1 to 2 inches (2.5 to 5 cm) in diameter. The color of the stalk ranges from almost white to yellow to deep green, red, or violet.

About 30 percent of sugarcane sap is sucrose. During harvesting, the cane stalks are stripped of leaves and trimmed for easier handling. In the factory, the stalks are washed and cut into short lengths or shredded.

Workers harvest sugarcane.

The sugar is removed from the canes by a diffusion process, in which the finely cut stalks are dissolved in hot water, or by milling, which entails pressing the stalks between heavy rollers to squeeze out the juice. In the latter process, the rollers are arranged in sets of three, each set exerting a greater pressure than the previous one. Water is sprayed on the stalks as they pass through the rollers to help dissolve additional juice. The waste material remaining after the rolling is called bagasse.

The acidic liquid extracted from cane is dark gray or greenish and contains impurities that need to be clarified by the use of chemicals. Milk of lime (a mixture of calcium hydroxide and water) is added to the juice, which is immediately heated to the boiling point and then run into settling tanks, where the precipitated matter is separated from the clear juice. To produce white sugar directly from the cane juice, sulfur dioxide and sometimes phosphoric acid are added to the juice before the milk of lime.

The juice is evaporated into a thick syrup and then concentrated by vacuum boiling in several stages. The vacuum allows the mixture to boil at

The Portvale sugar factory in Saint James is one of the largest cane-grinding factories on the island. A by-product of the sugarcane industry is rum.

THE MORGAN LEWIS SUGAR MILL

This huge stone mill is one of only two intact and restored sugar mills surviving in the Caribbean. It is typical of the wind-driven mills that crushed sugarcane for two centuries and produced the commodity that once made Barbados one of Britain's most valuable possessions in the Americas. The machinery that ground the cane is intact, but the canvas sails that caught the wind and turned the grinding mechanism are no longer on the arms.

a relatively low temperature, which prevents the syrup from scorching. It is boiled until sugar crystallizes out of the liquid, forming a mixture known as massecuite. Centrifugal machines (perforated hollow cylinders that revolve rapidly) separate the raw sugar crystals from the massecuite.

FISHING

The fishing industry, which had been in decline since the mid-1980s, has improved in recent years. In 1983 new and expanded facilities opened at the main fishing port of Oistins, and small boats are increasingly being replaced by larger and more powerful boats with large ice-storage chests that enable fishermen to stay at sea longer. More than 700 fishing vessels are used during the peak fishing season.

Closer to shore, reef fish are caught by simple lines from open boats or trapped in cagelike fish pots. Along the shore, nets of varying sizes are cast for fish such as fray, sprat, and pilcher.

A flying-fish vendor in Bridgetown.

Traditional fishermen in Oistins. The government is helping fishermen to upgrade to larger boats that can fish in waters farther from the island.

TRAINING FOR FISHERMEN The Fisheries Department conducts introductory training programs to teach fishermen to operate fishing vessels. It also plans to acquire a simulated wheelhouse, marine engines, and possibly its own fishing vessel, which can be used not only for training but also for marine science and exploratory and experimental fishing.

FLYING FISH Despite its name, the flying fish does not fly. It can, however, glide considerable distances by using its four "wings" (pectoral and ventral fins). Although 13 species of flying fish are found in the waters surrounding Barbados, only one species, *Hirundichthys affinis*, is caught commercially. In May, when the fish spawn, they can be scooped aboard by using a dip net. Flying fish account for 60 percent of all fish caught by commercial fishermen, and Barbados has often been called the Land of the Flying Fish.

A rum-bottling plant in Bridgetown.

MANUFACTURING

Manufacturing accounts for some 7 percent of Barbados's GDP and provides jobs for about 10,000 people. Electronic components, clothing, cement, furniture, medical supplies, and processed food are some of the products manufactured in Barbados.

MINING

The limestone that covers more than two-thirds of the island contains few impurities and is well suited for the manufacture of cement and the production of slaked lime for the iron, steel, and chemical industries. Some limestone locations produce what is locally called soft stone, traditionally used in the building industry for making blocks.

Closed for six years, the Arawak Cement Company plant reopened in 1997. It is now back to 80 percent capacity, having undergone a comprehensive restructuring program. At full capacity, the plant can produce 6,500 tons (6,604 metric tons) of cement a week. To protect the environment, systems such as dust extraction guarantee that the operation has only a small effect on the environment. Orimulsion, a low-emission fuel, is used to fire the kiln.

Sand is mined for the production of green and amber glass and for the building industry. Modern houses in Barbados are often built from cement or sandstone blocks.

FOREIGN TRADE

Sugar and its by-products, rum and molasses, together with electrical/ electronic components, clothing, and chemicals, are the country's chief exports. Main imports include machinery, food and beverages, fuel, and automobiles. The United States, the United Kingdom, and Trinidad and Tobago are Barbados's top trading partners.

ENERGY

Barbados produces natural gas and crude oil, the latter accounting for a third of the country's requirements. The Mobil Oil Refinery closed in 1998, and now

In 2008 Barbados had 2.2 million barrels of oil reserves. Stepped-up exploration, if successful, could boost this figure considerably.

Drilling for oil in Saint Philip.

The Barbados dollar is tied to the U.S. dollar at an approximate rate of Bds$2 to US$1. Other foreign currencies fluctuate daily against that standard. Barbadian notes come in the following denominations: Bds$2 (blue), Bds$5 (green), Bds$10 (brown), Bds$20 (purple), Bds$50 (orange), and Bds$100 (gray). Coins are in the denominations of Bds$1 and 1, 5, 10, and 25 cents.

the local crude oil produced is exported to Trinidad to be refined and then returned for domestic consumption.

Production of petroleum started at Woodbourne in Saint Philip in 1972. The oil fields were nationalized in 1982, and a national petroleum corporation was set up to implement public policy on crude-oil and natural-gas production. In late 1996 the Barbados National Oil Company signed an

Public transportation is comprehensive and inexpensive in Barbados.

agreement with a U.S. company to step up exploration activity, with the aim of making the country self-sufficient in energy. Since 2001 oil production has declined slightly. In 2003 the island's more than 100 wells produced about 365,000 barrels of crude oil.

Barbados's solar radiation levels, estimated at 3,200 calories per square inch (500 calories per square cm) per day, are among the highest in the world. Solar energy has been commercially available since 1974, providing a substitute for natural gas and imported energy. More than 20,000 houses in Barbados have solar panels on their roofs. A wind turbine at Lamberts in Saint Lucy also provides electricity to the Barbados Light and Power Company.

Bagasse, a by-product of the sugar industry, is an important source of biomass fuel and is used primarily to meet the energy requirements of sugarcane processing.

TRANSPORTATION

A network of major highways, all beginning at Bridgetown, spans the island. Driving time from Bridgetown to the east coast has been greatly reduced with the completion of the trans-insular highway, which cuts across the island. Public transportation is excellent, with government-operated Barbados Transport Board buses, privately run minibuses, and individually owned minivan cabs. Minibuses are perhaps the most popular form of transportation, as they are usually better maintained than government buses and less crowded than minivans. Virtually any place on the island can be reached by public bus, as buses cover the entire extensive paved-road network on regular schedules. There is also a helicopter shuttle service that provides air-taxi services to a number of sites on the island, mainly on the west coast tourist belt.

Barbados's only international airport, the Grantley Adams International Airport, is 8 miles (13 km) east of Bridgetown. It is served by several international airlines, including Caribbean Airlines, British Airways, American Airlines, and Air Canada. Miami is about three hours and thirty minutes away by air and New York five hours.

The port of Bridgetown was dredged in 2002 to allow safe access for many of the largest British, Continental European, and American cruise ships in the world. The number of cruise-ship passengers arriving in Barbados has been increasing steadily. By 2008, passenger arrivals had reached 597,523.

A train service, now discontinued, operated from Bridgetown from 1881 to 1938, linking places such as Bath, Martin's Bay, Bathsheba, and Belleplaine. The journey to Bathsheba often took three to four hours, depending on the condition of the railroad, which was sometimes obstructed by landslides.

Workers carry out some surveying work on a road.

ENVIRONMENT

The shore at Sandy Lane in Saint James.

CHAPTER **5**

THE COASTLINE OF BARBADOS AND its coral reefs and fishery are critical to the country, as they provide not only food but also employment through fishing, transportation, tourism, and recreation.

The marine areas and coral reefs are not as healthy as they once were due to domestic sewage, sediments from the construction industry and agriculture, and other pollutants that have seeped into the sea. Removal and infilling of mangrove swamps, such as Holetown Hole, have

Crane beach in Saint Lawrence.

destroyed important nursery areas for fish. The most pressing environmental problem is the uncontrolled handling of solid wastes, which can contaminate the water supply. Despite the pollution issues, 100 percent of Barbados's urban and rural populations have safe water.

COASTAL ZONE MANAGEMENT

Barbados is one of the world's most densely populated countries. Most of the island's population and economic activities are located within a narrow coastal band. The coastal zone is extremely important to the economy of the island. Coastal development, however, has damaged the coastline and the adjacent marine zone. The Coastal Zone Management Act was introduced in 1998 to coordinate and update the existing statutes relevant to coastal management and make provisions for the protection of coral and other marine reserves.

A diver explores the corals living on the shipwrecked *Stavronikita*, at Folkstone Marine Park just off Holetown.

REEF BALLS

Reef balls are man-made, individually created, specially treated concrete modules designed to attract marine life to a specific area. They can be used in any combination of numbers and sizes and are environmentally friendly, with a lifespan of approximately 500 years. The Barbados Marine Trust placed 30 reef balls into the water along the southern coast to create an artificial coral reef to mimic the natural environment, encourage the growth of new corals, and attract fish to the area. The Tourism Development Cooperation of Barbados donated $27,000 for the scientific monitoring and development of the reef-ball site. Many species of fish and coral have already established themselves at the site, including parrotfish, sergeants major, ocean sturgeons, and trumpetfish.

The government of Barbados is committed to ensuring that the island's coastal waters are maintained and protected from pollutants. The Marine Pollution Control Act of 1998 facilitates the prevention, reduction, and control of pollution of the marine environment from every possible source.

The Fisheries (Management) Regulations Act of 1998 is in place to protect the marine environment and to prevent overfishing. It covers issues such as permissible mesh size on nets and forbids the use of entangling nets. It also prohibits the capture of lobsters carrying eggs and the removal of eggs from lobsters, as well as the capture, possession, or sale of turtles, turtle eggs, and turtle parts. In addition, the act makes it illegal to land a tuna with a live weight of less than 7.05 pounds (3.2 kg), and it protects coral and aquatic flora from being harvested for ornamental purposes. Fines or a prison sentence of up to two years may be imposed if these or similar regulations are broken.

Barbados's main environmental agencies are the Ministry of Housing, Lands, and Environment, established in 1978, and the Barbados Water Authority, established in 1980. These agencies are responsible for addressing Barbados's primary environmental issues, which include coastal pollution from oil slicks and soil erosion, particularly in the northeast. In 1981 a marine reserve was created to protect the coastline. The Barbados Marine Trust is a nongovernmental organization dedicated to promoting environmentally and socially sustainable use of the marine areas of Barbados.

ENDANGERED SPECIES

There are a few endangered species in Barbados, including the Orinoco crocodile, the tundra peregrine falcon, the Eskimo curlew, and the Barbados yellow warbler. The Barbados raccoon has become extinct. Hawksbill sea turtles are critically endangered globally, and the most serious threat to their existence is from humans.

The beach between Coconut Court and the Hilton Hotel on Barbados is one of the most important hawksbill nesting beaches in the southern Caribbean. As hotels tend to remove vegetation from the beach in front of them, goat's foot yam and sea grape were planted in specific areas to try to encourage the turtles back to nest and lay eggs. Dwarf coconuts have been planted to block the residual light from the hotels, as turtles like to nest on dark beaches.

One of the most important nesting sites for the globally endangered hawksbill sea turtle is on Barbados.

Volunteers patrol the beach at night to stop poachers. The experiment has been successful, and hawksbill turtles have been nesting in these specially created areas since 2001, proving that with proper management, endangered hawksbill turtles stand a good chance of survival in the future.

The Barbados National Trust has established a replanting program to save the Barbados mastic tree. The tree has been harvested as an invaluable source of timber since the arrival of the Europeans. It is indigenous to the Caribbean, but intensive harvesting and habitat destruction have made the tree extremely scarce. The sole remaining wild tree on the island was spotted in 1989, growing on the roadside where it was brushed by passing cars and polluted by exhaust fumes and where any road-widening scheme would mark its demise. Seeds from this one remaining tree have been collected and germinated, and the resulting plants are being grown in protected public sites on the island, including at the Andromeda Botanic Gardens and Welchman Hall Gully.

WASTE DISPOSAL

The protection and enhancement of the environment is essential for the maintenance of good health. It has been estimated that every person generates about 2 pounds (0.9 kg) of solid waste each day. This amounts to an estimated island total of 443 tons (450 metric tons) a day, or 163,880 tons (166,510 metric tons) of solid waste every year. Organic matter accounts for 33 percent, nonorganic matter 26 percent, paper 20 percent, and plastic 9 percent of all wastes. Barbados is very concerned about the threats that this amount of waste can pose to the environment.

Currently only a small percentage of waste is recycled. The remaining waste is disposed of at landfill waste sites. These landfill sites must be carefully constructed and monitored to ensure that no pollutants leak into the surrounding ground. Unfortunately some residents and businesses do not adhere to proper waste-disposal practices. Plastic is not biodegradable, so if thrown on the roadside or into a gully it is likely to eventually wash into the sea, where it not only will be unsightly but will also add to coastal pollution and be hazardous for marine life.

The Mangrove Pond landfill site was the first in Barbados to be fitted with a clay liner and a leachate-collection system. Even so, there have been issues over the years concerning fires and offensive odors at this site. Recently the management of the landfill has improved considerably, but this site is nearing the end of its life span. A new landfill site at Greenland, despite many problems associated with its construction, will replace the Mangrove Pond site.

The Bagatelle bulky-waste landfill site is used for the disposal of waste such as building materials, rubble, scrap, automobiles, old appliances, and other noncombustible items. These items do not produce unpleasant odors or large amounts of leachate with contaminants of health or environmental concern, so the requirements and constraints for disposing of bulky waste are not as stringent as those for other types of wastes.

ILLEGAL DUMPING

Dumping of garbage in gullies or at the roadside is illegal and dangerous because it can contaminate the water supply and lead to diseases such as dengue fever and leptospirosis. Garbage dumped indiscriminately can also be a hazard to birds, fish, and other wildlife. The Barbados Environmental Association has estimated that more than 60 percent of the island's gullies are affected by illegal dumping. Some of these gullies are literally overflowing with the dumping of residential, agricultural, and commercial refuse. Even the roadside vendors of coconuts have been known to dump piles of coconut husks on the roadside or in fields instead of disposing of them properly. The government has implemented a public education program to raise awareness of the problems that illegal dumping can cause and thereby encourage people to dump garbage in a responsible manner in the allocated places or to telephone the Sanitation Service Authority to arrange collection of items such as large furniture, tree stumps, and major household appliances that are not collected by the solid-waste collection trucks.

LANDSLIDES AND SOIL EROSION

Between 1901 and 2000 Barbados suffered from eight landslides. These hazards were limited to the Scotland District, a region on the central east coast that consists of Saint Andrew Parish, most of Saint Joseph Parish, and part of Saint John Parish. The area covers one-seventh of the island and is made up of alternating beds of weak sandstone and shale that is highly weathered. Heavy rainfall increases groundwater instability, which in turn causes slope movement. In 1901 there was a landslip in Boscobel when heavy rain resulted in the movement of a 642-acre (260-ha) piece of land, destroying approximately 80 homes. The Scotland District Conservation Scheme, established in 1957, was set up to address the issue of soil erosion, and as a result several communities have been relocated to less susceptible areas of the island.

Soil erosion caused part of the road to fall away.

POLLUTION FROM SHIPPING

Pollution from the growing number of cruise ships, oil tankers, and other vessels visiting the island poses an increasing threat to the health and prosperity of Barbados. Shipping can harm the environment as a result of accidents in which oil and other pollutants are released or even as a result of irresponsible actions by the ships' captains or owners. Cruise ships, with around 3,000 people on board, generate a lot of waste on a daily basis. Apart from oil, wastes include dirty water from dishwashers and clothes washers, sewage, plastic, paper, glass, and toxic substances such as tributyltin (TBT), a key ingredient in antifouling marine paint, and chemicals from film processing. These may enter the sea with an accumulative impact on people, coral reefs and other wildlife, and the scenic beauty of the coastline that attracts tourists in the first place. There have been quantities of tar balls, the result of oil spills and discharge, found on the windward beaches of Barbados.

WATER MANAGEMENT

Household and industrial waste contaminating the water supply is a real threat, and decreasing quantities of freshwater for agriculture and drinking are a major concern, with Barbados officially listed as a "water-scarce country." Tourism, which brings a large number of visitors to the island, creates more of a problem, as do tourist facilities such as golf courses that need plenty of water. Tourist resorts use more water than comparable residential areas, so the use of water needs to be carefully managed.

Bananas, a crop that is important to Barbados, need a lot of water and are prone to black sigatoka disease under dry conditions. Global warming could therefore affect the agriculture of Barbados, although the main crop, sugarcane, is not particularly thirsty.

A high volume of cruise ships stop over in Barbados, generating a lot of waste.

CLIMATE CHANGE

A reduction in the amount of rainfall could aggravate the water shortage. Experts predict that rainfall may decrease by 4 percent in the coming years unless drastic cuts in greenhouse gas emissions occur. Barbados is active in attempting to overcome the potential water shortage by using advanced technologies such as reverse osmosis to obtain freshwater from seawater.

INTERNATIONAL ENVIRONMENTAL AGREEMENTS

Barbados is party to a number of international environmental agreements, namely Biodiversity, Climate Change, Climate Change—Kyoto Protocol, Desertification, Endangered Species, Hazardous Wastes, Law of the Sea, Marine Dumping, Ozone Layer Protection, Ship Pollution, and Wetlands.

OZZY OZONE

In 1997 Barbados sought to improve public awareness of the necessity to protect the ozone layer, and the character of Ozzy Ozone was born. A local artist created the printed cartoon series, but the government of Barbados holds the ownership and rights to the character.

Many public-awareness campaigns have been held, and Ozzy Ozone has been reproduced on posters, key rings, erasers, pencils, mouse pads, pens, stickers, rulers, and refrigerator magnets. Ozzy was so successful in Barbados that the character is now used globally by the United Nations Environment Program (UNEP) in its ozone awareness activities, which include producing educational items for global distribution. In 2004 UNEP released a video in which Ozzy explains the threats to the ozone layer and shows children how they can protect themselves from the effects of ultraviolet radiation caused by ozone depletion. Nearly 65 governments broadcast this video on Ozone Day (September 16), reaching millions of viewers. It has been translated from English into 24 languages. The character of Ozzy is still used worldwide to spread the message on ozone layer protection.

BARBADIANS

A young Barbadian boy.

WITH A POPULATION OF 284,589 living on just 166 square miles (431 square km) of land, Barbados is one of the most densely populated countries in the world.

More than 70 percent of Barbadians are direct descendants of slaves from Africa. Another 20 percent are of mixed black and white heritage, while 7 percent are white, with traditional Caucasian features and skin tone, or with a small amount of black ancestry. The remaining 3 percent are mostly members of immigrant groups from South America and Asia. Barbadians are thus a multiethnic people, with Afro-Bajans,

Schoolchildren in Saint John.

Anglo-Bajans of English or Scottish descent, Euro-Bajans, Bajan Jews, Bajan Muslims, Bajan Hindus, and even Arab-Bajans from Syria and Lebanon.

Forty percent of the population live in the urban region that stretches along the sheltered west coast of the island from Speightstown in the north to Oistins in the southeast. The remainder live in numerous villages and hamlets, ranging in size from 100 to 3,000 people, scattered throughout the countryside. More than 100,000 people live in the parish of Saint Michael alone, the majority of them in the capital city of Bridgetown.

SOCIAL HIERARCHIES

Barbados changed as the original forest cover was replaced by fields of sugarcane, and the island became densely settled. The landed elite considered itself an aristocracy. Below this plantocracy in the social structure were hundreds of small-farm families, traditionally called the yeomanry. Below them was a class

A shell seller.

of wage laborers, peasants, and unemployed vagrants made up of white indentured servants who had been displaced by black slavery.

Although intermarriages were few, interracial relationships between white planters and black slaves were common. A mulatto population grew on the island, creating a new class of Bajans who were usually better treated than the blacks. White fathers often had their mulatto children baptized and freed from slavery.

A wide gap between the very wealthy (white plantocracy) and the very poor (black plantation slaves) has always existed. Although this gap has narrowed since the days of slavery, the contrast between the luxurious mansions of the wealthy and the small chattel houses of the poor remains enormous, as does the difference in lifestyles.

HIGH WHITES The island's history and economic development have been dominated by about 20 families who still rank among Barbados's elite today. The great wealth of these families was built on growing sugarcane on huge plantations. The island (which they called Bimshire) was their home, and unlike other West Indian planters, very few of these plantation owners were absentee landlords. Instead they assumed the role of lord of the manor and re-created patterns of English country life. Today many of their houses bear British names, and they continue to dominate the commercial and economic life of the island.

RED LEGS Before the slave trade brought African blacks to Barbados to work on the sugar plantations, the island's labor force consisted of

Children playing outside the Mount Gay Rum plant. Whites are a minority in Barbados.

white indentured servants, many of whom were inmates of English jails and royalists who had been captured and imprisoned during the English civil war.

The contracts of the indentured servants were sold to planters on arrival in Barbados, where the conditions of their servitude were often no better than slavery. When their indentures ended, some left the island. Those who remained lived in villages on the inhospitable eastern side of the island, where they survived by fishing and hunting turtles and crabs.

Sometimes planters, embarrassed to see them so destitute, provided schools, jobs, and even clubs for them. To keep the poor whites in the city from delinquency, the Young Men's Progressive Club (YMPC) was established in the 1920s. There they could play cricket, soccer, and indoor games, attend lectures, and benefit from cultural programs. The earliest Caribbean literary magazine, *Bim*, was started by Frank Collymore and Therold Barnes, early

Bajan children laughing and joking.

members of the YMPC and both descendants of poor whites. Today Bajan poor whites are a small and vanishing minority that is being assimilated into the middle class.

MIXED MARRIAGES

In the past, white planters often had a relationship with a black mistress or "outside" woman, but accepting blacks or mulattoes socially was another matter, and racial discrimination was practiced in commerce and in the civil service. Today, although attitudes are changing, Bajan whites and blacks, as a rule, do not marry one another. Most of the interracial couples seen on the island are foreigners.

BAJAN BLACKS

The planters encouraged their African slaves to raise large families, and the population on the island eventually became overwhelmingly Creole. Of mixed black and European ancestry, these Bajan Creoles gained the reputation of being the most loyal slaves in the West Indies. Nevertheless, the two world wars in the 20th century gave hundreds of Bajan blacks an opportunity to view life from a different perspective overseas. When these Bajan blacks returned home, many helped organize workers and unions to improve their working conditions. The success of blacks in sports, especially cricket, also renewed their pride in their black heritage.

By the 1960s politicians who had spent part of their life abroad were proud to be black and Bajan. Leaders such as Errol Barrow, who had been a World War II airman and trained in London as a lawyer and economist,

A young girl in Bridgetown.

The following excerpt from Bruce St. John's Bumbatuk 1 *reveals the sense of unity and national pride that exists in Barbados today:*

All o'we is Bajan!
Bajan to de backbone ...
Bajan black, Bajan white,
Bajan hair curly, Bajan hair straight,
Yo' brother red, yo' sister brown
Yo' mother light-skin, yo' father cob skin ...

and Sir Grantley Adams, another London-trained lawyer, worked toward independence for Barbados. Sir Arleigh Winston Scott, a Bajan black who had trained as a doctor in the United States, in 1967 became the first native governor-general of Barbados.

NEW BAJANS

The influx of Indians, Pakistanis, and Lebanese as well as immigrants from the United States, Canada, Great Britain, Germany, South America, and even China has stirred modern Bajan blacks to insist on respect for their hard-won culture. African traditions and folklore have been resurrected, and schoolchildren are encouraged to read the African-inspired poetry of Eddie Kamau Brathwaite and the writings of George Lamming, Bruce St. John, and others who have explored the meanings of being Bajan in literary forms.

DRESS

Most Barbadians are stylish but conservative in their dress. Women vendors in the marketplaces, for example, often favor old-fashioned, matronly dresses and tie their hair up in handkerchiefs. Office workers, on the other hand, are often seen in high heels and tailored dresses or skirts and blouses. Skimpy clothes are frowned on in towns and are usually seen only at beach areas.

Even in the most rural areas, schoolchildren, both boys and girls, wear uniforms of pressed shirts and ties, with girls wearing their hair neatly braided and tied with color-coded ribbons. For social events such as weddings and parties, Barbadians love to dress up, and they always wear their Sunday best for church meetings.

SOME PROMINENT BARBADIANS

CRICKETERS One of the world's top players, Bajan national hero Sir Garfield Sobers was knighted by Queen Elizabeth II during her visit to Barbados in 1975. Another cricket hero, Sir Frank Worrell, who appears on the Bds$5 bill, was captain of the hugely successful West Indian team that toured Australia in 1960 and 1961. Worrell is buried in a prominently marked grave at the Cave Hill campus of the University of the West Indies.

A woman in traditional dress.

MUSICIANS Calypso artist Anthony Carter, better known as the Mighty Gabby, is famous for his songs of cultural identity and political protest that speak for emerging black pride throughout the Caribbean. Red Plastic Bag (born Stedson Wiltshire), also known as RPB or just Bag, is another calypsonian. He combines the sounds of soca and reggae, and his biggest hit, "Ragga Ragga," has been recorded in seven languages.

AUTHORS Frank Collymore is regarded as the founder of the Barbadian literary movement. George Lamming is an internationally recognized novelist and scholar.

LIFESTYLE

A street scene in Barbados.

CHAPTER 7

>CULTURAL INFLUENCES ON Barbados, with its British past, are a mixture of African and British heritage. The latter predominates in institutional ways, including the form of government, education, and legal framework, but African influences remain strong in family life and in music and dance.

Supportive networks of female relatives, such as sisters, mothers, and daughters, are especially strong. These networks sometimes include male relatives such as uncles, brothers, cousins, and grandfathers as

A Barbadian boy on his bicycle.

Barbados is a former British colony, and most Bajans are proud of their British past. The stoic British influence is evident, but the flamboyant African sway pervades local life as well. The people are fun-loving, flexible, adaptable, and well-educated. Festivals commemorate many significant events in the history and development of Barbados.

well. More than one-third of households in Barbados are headed by women, and the family home remains a place to which Barbadians can return at any time in their lives.

MARRIAGE

Many women enter into a number of unions before settling down to marriage. Couples may start with a "visiting union," where the woman lives with her parents and is visited by her male friend. Sometimes the couple move in together and eventually marry, but often they remain casual and eventually separate.

In addition to home and children, which are the main concerns for most women, marriage is an ultimate goal, even if the women have to wait many years. Bajan weddings were once grand affairs with no expense spared. Although elaborate receptions are no longer common because of the rising cost of living, weddings are still important celebrations for Barbadians.

Weddings are usually held in a church on a Saturday afternoon. The bride is usually dressed in white lace, satin, or chiffon and may have as many as eight bridesmaids. The groom and his best man put on stylish, dark suits with orchid boutonnieres.

A mother and child in Bridgetown. Family ties are very important to Barbadians.

After the ceremony, the wedding party drives in procession to the reception, where amid speech-making, the couple is toasted, and an elaborately decorated cake is served. This is usually followed by much dancing and feasting until about 11 P.M.

FAMILY LIFE

Couples usually lead relatively separate lives, even engaging in different leisure activities. Fathers may take an interest in their children's education, but most believe that their primary responsibility is to provide financial support, even if they no longer live with the children's mother. Family life is centered around the mother, who performs all the child-rearing tasks. Her relationship with her children is usually close and lasting.

Mothers take their responsibilities seriously. They are often strict disciplinarians, insisting on good manners and respect for elders. Children are taught to use appropriate greetings when passing people on the road or on entering shops. Three-generation households, especially those consisting of grandmother, mother, and children, are common in Barbados.

A Barbadian family walks home after attending Sunday service at the local church.

Couples in Barbados are now having fewer chidlren.

CHANGING PATTERNS

Today young couples are marrying earlier, and both usually continue working. Most rely on the grandmother to help out with their children, although a fortunate few may be able to afford a maid. Contraception, now generally accepted and easily available, limits the number of children.

DEATH

Regardless of their religious affiliation, most Bajans consider funeral attendance important. Funerals start at around 4 P.M. and follow a set ritual. The open coffin is placed near the entrance of the church. Close relatives stand on one side, while the other mourners file past the body. Pamphlets detailing hymns to be sung and other procedures to be followed are handed out. The coffin is then closed and wheeled farther into the church for the service, which includes hymns, prayers, the officiating priest's address, and a eulogy by a close friend of the deceased. As the last hymn is sung, the coffin is turned around and wheeled feet first to the door. Six pallbearers carry it to the cemetery or into a hearse, which leads a procession of vehicles to the cemetery.

Funerals are attended for a variety of reasons—the deceased might be a relative, a neighbor, a casual or job-related acquaintance, or a close friend. Ensuring that the funeral has a good turnout, especially if the death occurred in unusual circumstances, is important. The black and white clothes that were once required wear at funerals have been replaced by light colors. Wearing bright colors to a funeral, however, is considered a sign of disrespect. Nowadays a get-together is usually held after the funeral, during which a variety of food and drink is served. There is no dancing or music, but loud talk and laughter may continue for several hours, serving to relieve temporarily the sadness of the bereaved.

Some Barbadians believe that the dead can convey messages to their kin through dreams. They hold wakes called nine-nights to ensure that the soul has a safe journey to the next world. They may also conduct ceremonies to communicate with the dead in the hope that the dead will rectify problems they may have caused while alive.

HOUSING

Some 70 percent of houses in Barbados are occupied by the owners. Almost all households have running water, 80 percent have televisions and refrigerators, and 55 percent have telephones. Modern houses are often built from concrete. Many new residential estates for the middle class have sprung up, where satellite dishes and solar panels on the roof are not unusual.

Chattel houses, which were traditionally home to slaves, can still be found in many parts of the island. These were designed to be taken apart and moved, if necessary, as slaves were not allowed to own land. The foundations usually consist of stones, and the walls of the houses are weathered planks. Traditionally each window has three wooden shutters called jalousies, two hinged at the sides and one hinged from above to allow for flexibility in adjusting to sun and wind. Some chattel houses look weather-beaten and neglected, while others have been given a fresh coat of bright-colored paint.

Barbados also has several plantation houses, most of which have been taken over by the Barbados National Trust. The lifestyle that created these grand homes no longer exists on the island, and the houses are now mainly of historical interest.

Saint Nicholas Abbey in the parish of Saint Peter is the oldest house on the island and one of only three remaining examples of Jacobean architecture in the Americas. The house is believed to have been built in the 1650s. The

A house in Bridgetown.

interior, filled with beautiful antiques and paintings, offers a glimpse of plantation life during those early years.

Drax Hall in the parish of Saint George is another fine example of Jacobean architecture. The plantation, one of the first to cultivate sugarcane on a large scale, is the only estate to have stayed in the same family since the 17th century. Sunbury Plantation House in the parish of Saint Philip is now a museum, with a unique collection of plantation artifacts and tools, such as antique plows and cane carts, on its grounds.

EDUCATION

Barbadians have one of the highest literacy rates in the world, estimated at 99.7 percent. School attendance is compulsory for all children between

Saint Nicholas Abbey is more than 300 years old.

Boys learning how to use the computer in school.

the ages of five and 16, and all government schools, both elementary and secondary, are free.

ELEMENTARY SCHOOLS About 28,000 pupils attend the 85 elementary schools in Barbados. Children under five years of age go to nursery school. Elementary school pupils graduate to secondary school when they reach the age of 11. Regardless of their social and economic background, all children in elementary school receive low-cost meals supplied by the government.

SECONDARY SCHOOLS Some 22,000 students between the ages of 11 and 18 are enrolled in the 23 government secondary schools, where the trend is toward a coeducational system. Another 3,000 students attend government-approved private secondary schools.

An elementary school class in Saint James.

SPECIAL SCHOOLS Special schools on the island include two government residential industrial schools, which provide training for slow learners; a school for the deaf; a school for the blind; and the Challenor School for the mentally challenged. The Challenor School was on the verge of closure in 2006, but funds were received, renovations were made, and the school reopened as a state-of-the-art facility for both children and adults.

HIGHER EDUCATION A coeducational teachers' training college, opened in 1948, provides training for graduate and nongraduate teachers. The Samuel Jackman Prescod Polytechnic has more than 2,000 students. Training is provided for the electrical, building, and engineering trades; commercial and agricultural studies; and human ecology, which includes cosmetology and home economics. The Barbados Community College offers a

A hospital in Bridgetown. Barbadians enjoy a high standard of health care.

wide range of academic, vocational, and technical programs, including fine arts, health sciences, liberal arts, and science.

The government also pays the fees of all Barbadians at the Cave Hill campus of the University of the West Indies, which offers courses in arts, natural sciences, social sciences, and law, as well as advanced education for adults at the extramural center. The Cave Hill campus is linked to the university's three other campuses, in Jamaica, Trinidad, and the Bahamas, via a telecommunications network that allows teleconferencing and distance teaching. Barbados also has several secretarial colleges and language institutes.

HEALTH

Barbadians enjoy a high standard of health care. Several government polyclinics offer health services, including maternity and child care, family planning, health education, school health services, control of communicable diseases, and environmental health. The Winston Scott Polyclinic, the island's largest polyclinic, has facilities for X-rays, yellow-fever surveillance, bacteriological analysis, and food testing, as well as an eye clinic and a skin-disease center. Treatment and medication at these walk-in clinics are free for all Bajans.

ALTERNATIVE MEDICINE

Although modern medicine has superseded traditional folk cures, many Bajans still turn to the indigenous plants and herbs originally used in teas and cures by the early migrants and to the bush medicine brought over from Africa by their ancestors.

The Rastafarian movement also prefers natural cures, which has extended the range of Barbadian folk medicine. Coconut water, sold by Rastafarians on street corners, is regarded as a preventative and a cure for illnesses of the kidney and the bladder. Similarly, coconut oil can be rubbed on the head to break up a cold or into the scalp to loosen dandruff two days before washing the hair.

The pawpaw, as the papaya is known on the island, has many uses. It helps bowel movement and can help reduce hypertension, or high blood pressure, when eaten green, in two small, cooked slices. To prevent infection, Bajans apply several thin slices over a cut and then bandage them into place for two or three days.

The cactuslike aloe plant also has many uses. To ease colds, irritated throats, and constipation, a small piece of the inner pith is swallowed with a pinch of salt. Aloe slices can be bandaged onto cuts to aid healing, and for sunburn one side of a piece of aloe is peeled and the cool inside is rubbed over the affected area. It is extremely soothing and can even stop the skin from peeling.

Many Bajans still abide by and turn to alternative medicine.

A bitter green brew made from the circee bush is used to reduce fevers and relieve influenza symptoms. Wonder-of-the-world, when chewed with a pinch of salt, is believed to relieve mild attacks of asthma.

RELIGION

Saint Michael's Anglican Cathedral.

IN THE EARLY DAYS, DESPITE AN official policy of religious tolerance, Catholics, Jews, and nonconformist Protestants were discriminated against and kept from all seats of political power.

Anglican clergymen were an important element in the plantocracy that dominated public life and all civic organizations, fashioning social ideologies based on white, Anglo-Saxon Anglicans. It was not until 1797 that Anglican ministers were allowed to offer slaves some religious training. Later, Anglican religious training became part of the preparation for emancipation.

Worshipers in Saint Peter's church.

There are more than 100 established religions on the island of Barbados, and most families attend some type of religious gathering at least once a week. Most Christians go to church. The Anglican churches established in the 17th century are some of the largest places of worship on the island, but some gatherings take place in halls or even houses.

Children at Sunday school.

Today some 40 percent of the population is Anglican. Other denominations such as Methodists, Moravians, and Roman Catholics are well represented. In addition, there are followers of more than 100 other religions, denominations, and sects in Barbados, such as Rastafarians, Jews, Muslims, and Hindus.

ANGLICANS

After centuries as the official religion in Barbados, the Anglican Church still enjoys the widest following among Barbadians. Its parish churches once dominated rural life, but this is less true today. Anglicans in Barbados are adherents of the Church in the Province of the West Indies.

OTHER CHRISTIAN FAITHS

METHODISM The first Methodist missionaries arrived in Barbados in the late 18th century and initially struggled to spread their faith in the face of repression. In 1823 their church was destroyed, and proclamations threatening to abolish Methodism were posted in Bridgetown. Led by Ann Gill, however, the Methodists resisted. After the Emancipation Act was passed, Methodist ranks were swelled by the newly freed slaves. Today there are more than 20 Methodist churches on the island.

MORAVIANISM The Moravian Church is the oldest Protestant religion in the world. The church became known for supporting slaves under its leader Benjamin Brookshaw, and in 1816 its members were granted virtual immunity from the terror of the slave revolt. Today Moravians in Barbados are predominantly black.

ROMAN CATHOLICISM   Similar to the other non-Anglican faiths, Catholicism was suppressed in Barbados before the 19th century. The first Catholic church in Barbados was built in 1848. Catholics are a small minority on the island.

TIE-HEADS

Locals refer to the followers of the indigenous Apostolic Spiritual Baptist religion, founded by Bishop Granville Williams in 1957, as Tie-Heads. They wear colorful gowns of different hues symbolizing particular qualities, and all tie cloths around their heads. During services lively music is accompanied by foot stomping, hand clapping, and dancing.

RASTAFARIANS

The Rastafarian movement began in Jamaica in the 1920s when Marcus Garvey advocated a back-to-Africa ideal and urged his followers to "look to Africa, when a black king shall be crowned, for the day of deliverance is at hand." Then in Ethiopia in 1930, Ras Tafari, who claimed to be a direct descendant of King David and the 225th in an unbroken line of Ethiopian kings from the time of Solomon and Sheba, was crowned Emperor Haile Selassie I, "King of Kings, Lord of Lords, and the Conquering Lion of the Tribe of Judah." This last title inspired the dreadlocks and the strutting walk by which Rastafarians became identified.

Introduced in Barbados in 1975, the movement spread quickly and for a time attracted undesirable elements, such as criminals and rebellious youths who used it as an excuse to smoke marijuana, which is considered a sacrament among Rastafarians. This made the movement unpopular with

Rastafarians can usually be distinguished by their dreadlocks. They stress the need to regain pride in their black heritage by leading peaceful, pious lives engaged in contemplation, while rejecting the white man's world.

more conservative Barbadians. In due course, however, the fad died down, and some of the remaining Rastafarians have made names for themselves in sports and the arts.

FOLK BELIEFS

The lack of Christian missionaries in the early days enabled slaves to retain African folk beliefs and superstitions, some of which still exist.

- Obeah, a form of witchcraft believed to have originated from a West African religion called Obi, is now limited to a small number of people who believe in its power. Come-to-me sauce is an obeah potion believed to make the woman who administers it irresistibly attractive to her victim. Stay-at-home sauce is said to discourage husbands from straying.
- *Duppies* (DOO-pees), or spirits of the dead, are supposed to roam the earth at night. To prevent them from entering homes, people hang herbs in the windows and doorways and scatter sand around the house. This forces the *duppy* to stop and count each grain, which keeps him busy until daylight. Sprinkling a few drops from a new rum bottle on the ground for the spirits remains a Barbadian tradition. *Duppy* dust—grave dirt or pulverized human bones—is supposed to be fatal when thrown on a victim or put in his food.
- *Conrads* (KON-rads), or avenging ghosts, are said to take possession of their victims' bodies and shout nasty things in strange voices.
- *Baccoos* (bah-KOOS), bestowers of good or evil depending on the amount of attention they get, are tiny men said to often live in bottles.

Hags were especially ugly spirits, usually of planters' wives, who shed their skin and traveled about as balls of fire. If the skin was found and rubbed with pepper or salt, the hag would be unable to reenter it and would die.

PLACES OF WORSHIP

Saint Michael's Anglican Cathedral in Bridgetown dates from 1789. The original church, built in 1665 to accommodate 3,000 worshipers, was leveled by a hurricane a century later. The current cathedral seats 1,600. Many island notables are buried in the adjacent churchyard, including Sir Grantley Adams, first premier of Barbados and head of the West Indies

The restored Barbados Synagogue.

Federation from 1958 to 1962, and his son, Tom, who was prime minister from 1976 to 1985.

The original Barbados Synagogue in Bridgetown was built in 1654 by Jews from Recife, Brazil. Persecuted by the Dutch, they settled in Barbados and, being skilled in the sugar industry, quickly introduced the crop and passed on their skills to local landowners. The synagogue, destroyed by a hurricane in 1831, was rebuilt in 1833 but abandoned in 1929. The distinctive white building has recently been restored.

Saint James Parish Church, just north of the Holetown town center, is the site of the region's oldest church. The original church, built in 1660, was replaced by a more substantial structure in the mid-19th century, but a few vestiges of the original remain, including a bell inscribed with the name of King William cast in the late 1600s.

Other places of worship include the Emmanuel Baptist Church, the First Church of Christian Scientists, and the Roman Catholic Saint Patrick's Cathedral (all in Saint Michael), and the Anglican Saint Lawrence, the Methodist Hawthorne Memorial, the Bethlehem Moravian, and the Roman Catholic Saint Dominic's (all in Christ Church).

LANGUAGE

A traditionally dressed Barbadian woman chatting on a cell phone.

CHAPTER 9

T

HE OFFICIAL LANGUAGE OF Barbados is English. Bajan, however, is the dialect of the majority of the people. A combination of African languages and English, Bajan has taken time to mature to its current form.

Originally African expressions were translated literally into English but pronounced with African intonations. The English influence slowly became stronger, however.

Bajan, like other Caribbean dialects, became known as a Cinderella language—for a long time it was dismissed as the language of the

The most widely spoken language in Barbados is English, but many Bajans speak a dialect of the English language derived from their West African slave ancestors mixed with British English, resulting in the colorful and expressive dialect, or patois, called Bajan. Speech is fast paced, and many colorful turns of phrase are incorporated, which can make it hard to understand.

Two Bajan schoolgirls. The official language of Barbados is English but a common dialect is Bajan.

illiterate, restricted to the kitchen and the backyard. However, growing pride in black heritage and the emergence of Barbadian writers, poets, and linguists has proved that Bajan has a beauty of its own.

BAJAN

The following poem by Bruce St. John serves as an example of the Bajan language:

BAJAN	ENGLISH
We' language limit?	Is our language limited?
Who language en limit?	Whose language isn't limited?
Evah language	Every language
Like a big pot o' Bajan soup	Like a big pot of Bajan soup
Piece o' yam, piece o' potato	Piece of yam, piece of potato
T'ree dumplin', two eddoe	Three dumplings, two eddoes
One beet, two carrot	One beet, two carrots
Piece o' pig-tail, piece o' beef	Piece of pig-tail, piece of beef
Pinch o' salt, dus' o' pepper	Pinch of salt, dusting of pepper
An' don' fuget okra	And don't forget okra
To add to de flavor	To add to the flavor
Boil up, cook up, eat up	Boil it, cook it all together, eat it up
An' yuh still wan' rice	And you still want rice ...

From this comparison, the following can be deduced:
- In Bajan the same form of pronoun can be used as subject, object, or possessive: "we know," "tell we" (tell us), and "we language" (our language);
- a statement becomes a question only by the use of a different intonation; and
- endings such *as -ed* are left out, and in general, words often have the

boy, girl—*commonly used by islanders when addressing adults as well as children*

fire a grog, fire one—*drink rum*

go so, swing so—*used in giving directions (combined with hand movements that must be watched because they are a visual reference to the direction!)*

limin' *(also lime, lime about)*—*hanging out; relaxing*

no problem—*all-purpose response to any request*

one time—*immediately; right away*

study—*take time to consider; think about*

wine—*sensuous dance movement, winding the hips, essential to carnival dancing*

workin' up—*dancing in general*

last letter unpronounced, and no *s* needs to be added to indicate plurality.

There is no *th* sound in Bajan, and it can be replaced by any of the following: *f, v, t, d, z,* or *k:*

Breathe becomes	*breav*
With	*wit, wid,* or *wif*
Clothe	*cloze* or *clove*
Think	*t'ink*
The	*de*
Strengthen	*strengken* or *strengfen*

Bajans use the present tense even for past actions and express "habitual" actions by saying something "does" happen. Instead of using the word "very," Bajans say something is "pretty, pretty, pretty" or "real p-r-e-t-t-y," with great emphasis placed on the word *pretty*.

STORYTELLING TRADITION

Bajans love to entertain one another with ghost stories, and myths and legends from African sources are part and parcel of everyday conversation. Folktales and songs combine legend, history, religion, and local events and can be educational, as they often contain a moral, or purely entertaining, or sometimes both. The West African "Anancy" folktales inspired the phrase "nancy story," implying a tall tale or a lie. A mother might say to her children, "Don't give me no nancy story!"

The following is a Bajan folktale: A sick man visits a metaphysician in Bridgetown. The practitioner explains that pain and illness exist only in the mind, and all the sick person has to do to get well is to "affirm and believe" that the pain has gone. The sick man follows the practitioner's advice and recovers his health. When the practitioner asks for his fees, his patient tells him, "Wha' fees? All you have to do is affirm and believe dat you have receive de fees, and you have dem."

THE BARBADOS NATIONAL ANTHEM

Lyrics by Irving Burgie

In plenty and in time of need
When this fair land was young
Our brave forefathers sowed the seed
From which our pride is sprung
A pride that makes no wanton boast
Of what it has withstood
That binds our hands from coast to coast
The Pride of Nationhood

We loyal sons and daughters all
Do hereby make it known
These fields and hills beyond recall
Are now our very own
We write our name on history's page
With expectations great
Strict guardians of our heritage
Firm craftsmen of our fate.

The Lord has been the people's guide
For past three hundred years
With him still on the people's side
We have no doubts or fears
Upward and onward we shall go
Inspired, exciting, free
And greater will our nation grow
In strength and unity.

GREETINGS AND GESTURES

Barbadians consider it impolite not to greet someone with "good morning," "good afternoon," or "good evening" when passing him on the road or entering a shop. Handshakes and smiles are exchanged on meeting. Sometimes acquaintances will embrace one another. Bajans often wave their hands to greet a passing friend, while conversing to emphasize a point, or merely to call a passing taxi or bus. Folded arms indicate that complete attention is being given to the matter under discussion, but standing with hands on hips usually shows defiance. Puckered lips producing a *chupse* sound express disgust.

The public library in Bridgetown is more than 100 years old.

THE PUBLIC LIBRARY

In the early part of the 18th century, it was said that "everything was imported into Barbados except books." A Literary Society was established in 1777 and a Library Association in 1814, but both were private organizations for members only.

In 1847, three years before the first Public Libraries Act was passed in Britain, an act was passed in Barbados establishing a public library and museum on the island. However, the library was considered to be "miserably deficient in every branch of literature" by Greville John Chester, an English author and clergyman who spent some months on the island in 1867 and 1868. The current public library building on Bridgetown's Coleridge Street, paid for by the Scottish-American philanthropist Andrew Carnegie on condition that it should always be maintained as a free library, was opened in 1904.

Proverbs expressing folk values are constantly used in Bajan homes. Their commonsense wisdom is intended to instruct or admonish people in matters that occur frequently.

If greedy wait, hot will cool.	*Patience will get you what you want.*
One bellyful don' fattan a hog.	*Sustained effort is needed to achieve good results.*
Hungry mek cat eat salt.	*Necessity makes people do unusual things.*
De sea en' got no back door.	*The sea is not a safe place.*
Mek-sure better than cock-sure.	*Making sure is better than taking things for granted.*
Every skin teet' en' a laugh.	*Friendly smiles may not be genuine.*
Hansome don' put in pot.	*Physical beauty does not provide practical benefits.*

COMMUNICATIONS

Barbados is one of the most wired countries in the world when it comes to telephone infrastructure, telecommunications, and the Internet. The island has high-speed Internet access via wireless and ADSL. The main Internet service providers are Cable & Wireless, Sunbeach Communications, and TeleBarbados. In a 2009 report Internet usage was put at 66.1 percent of the population, not too far behind the United States at 73.9 percent of the population. In 2007 Barbados had 257,596 cell phones, or nearly one cell phone per adult. The two mobile service providers are Cable & Wireless and Digicel.

Barbados has its own television station, as well as access to satellite and cable channels, two major radio broadcasting companies, and four radio stations. Daily newspapers include *The Advocate* (established in 1895) and *The Nation*. Regional and international publications are also readily available.

ARTS

A mural of the Last Supper, painted on the side
of a Rastafarian home.

BARBADIANS ARE PROUD OF THEIR cultural heritage, a pride that is particularly evident in their music. For example, the songs of the island's most famous musician, the Mighty Gabby, are infused with a deep love for his homeland. Barbados also has a rich tradition of arts and crafts, literature, and architecture.

MUSIC

Caribbean music has its roots in African folk music and drumming, with some Spanish, French, and English influences. Reggae and calypso

Outdoor musicians draw a crowd.

The melding of African and British cultures in Barbados has created a distinctive and energetic culture with fine and colorful music, literature, art, crafts, and history. The vibrant art community explores many media, blending Afro-Caribbean and Western influences to create original work in all fields of the arts and crafts.

Gabby, whose real name is Tony Carter, began singing at the age of six and placed third in his first calypso competition in his teens. He spent a few years in New York, perfecting his writing and performing skills, and on his return to Barbados became the Barbadian equivalent of Jamaica's Bob Marley. He has also won recognition as folksinger of the year, and his music speaks for the thousands of Barbadians who see their culture as being under threat from foreign influence.

In "Culture," he sings:

> *All o' dem shows pon TV you must agree are not for we*
>
> *Show me some* Castle in My Skin *by George Lamming*
>
> *Instead of that trash like* Sanford *and* M*A*S*H
>
> *Then we could stare in the face*
>
> *And show dem we cultural base.*

are the two types of music heard most often, with their catchy, singable tunes blaring in minibuses and out of restaurants and beach bars. Soca, which blends soul with calypso, is dance music with bold rhythms. Heavy on the bass sounds, soca is heard most frequently during carnivals.

CALYPSO African slaves brought their songs to the West Indies beginning in the early 1600s. Plantation owners thought that beating drums and other loud instruments could encourage their slaves to revolt, so all such instruments were banned. But music remained a vital part of the Africans' daily life and could not be suppressed. The slaves sang while they worked, celebrated holidays with songs, and sang at funerals. This music, indigenous to Barbados, could only be performed in private, out of earshot of the plantation owners. After the slaves were emancipated in 1838, it survived only by becoming folk music.

Calypso, which originated in Trinidad, began influencing Barbadian folk music in the early 20th century. The songs from Trinidad increased the range of both melodies and lyrics, which changed from mere gossip and scandal

A man playing the steel pan. Each pan, or drum, is customed-designed.

to include satire and social commentary. Calypso was not taken seriously, however, and early singers were regarded as comics rather than serious performers. Talented Barbadian performers such as the Mighty Charmer and the Mighty Sugar were forced to move to Trinidad for recognition and to make their records. Eventually, in the 1960s and '70s, a group of white middle-class Barbadians called the Merrymen created a series of hits by combining folk and country music with Bajan calypso.

Contemporary calypso features biting social commentary, political satire, and sexual innuendo. Calypso competitions are now a major part of carnival festivities, with singers competing for the title of "king."

***TUK* BANDS** The *boom-a-tuk, boom-a-tuk* sound given out by the big log drum gives these bands their name. For more than 100 years, *tuk* (also known as *tuck* or *took*) music has been played at picnics and excursions and on public holidays. It is lively, with an intricate fast beat suggestive of English military bands. *Tuk* bands travel from village to village playing popular tunes and

A dance troupe performs during a festival.

encouraging the villagers to contribute their own compositions. People dress up in unusual clothes, and everyone joins in the dancing and fun. Traditional dancers such as the tiltman, who performs on very tall stilts, usually accompany tuk bands and solicit contributions from the audience.

STEEL DRUM (steel pan) Originally from Trinidad, the distinctive, melodious sounds of this music have spread throughout the Caribbean, including Barbados. It was created by musicians who took discarded oil drums and hammered out the steel bottom, tuning different sections to specific pitches. Drummers now play together in bands.

DANCE

It is said that most Bajans can dance before they can walk. When music fills the air, toddlers stand and sway to the rhythm of calypso. Early planters quickly realized that their slaves worked better when they were allowed to enjoy their own form of dancing and music once or twice a week. The dancers shout, clap their hands, and chant, twisting and turning energetically.

In recent years, after formal ballet became available to a larger number of Barbadians, modern dance techniques have developed, and folktales have inspired performances by groups such as the Barbados Dance Theater.

LANDSHIPS

The landship movement developed from early friendly societies—institutions that, for a small weekly payment, provided insurance for the sick as well as

The play 1627 and All That, *presented at the Sherbourne Conference Center, re-creates a 17th-century Barbadian ambience. The main event, a dramatization of 17th-century Barbadian life, is vividly performed by a troupe of energetic dancers.*

death benefits. Landships provided the working class with a social organization that satisfied their need for cultural expression as well as assistance for workers in times of need. Members of landships were ranked and defined in accordance with the hierarchy of the British navy. Meetings and parades displayed naval-style drills, uniforms, and disciplines.

Many communities developed their own landships in the 1920s. These competed in displays of discipline, uniform, drill, and other naval rituals. Today there are a half-dozen landships, and no big occasion in Barbados, from a state funeral to the Crop Over festivities, is complete without landship participation.

THEATER

Plantation improvisations called tea meetings in the 1600s provided entertainment in the form of enslaved Africans reciting passages and spontaneous speeches or performing slapstick skits for their own entertainment. Troupes of traveling actors would also give spontaneous open-air performances when their ships came into port. The first mention of theater in Barbados, however, appeared in George Washington's diary when he noted that he attended a presentation of *The Tragedy of George Barnwell* in 1751.

By 1783 a theater called Patagonian, which presented plays including those by Shakespeare, was facing competition from a rival theater called the New Theater, whose comedies and pantomimes drew large crowds. These audiences were made up exclusively of the white planter class. It was not until after World War II that nonwhites such as the Green Room Players began to stage productions of local and international plays.

A modern-day dinner theater production, *Barbados by Night*, at the Plantation Restaurant and Garden Theater provides a whirlwind of dance and energy, depicting the cultures of the Caribbean as influenced by the English, the French, the Spanish, and the Africans. It also features fire-eating limbo dancers and steel-band, reggae, and calypso music.

Constructed in 1854 by a local builder, William Farnum, the Tyrol Cot Great House is a restrained blend of Palladian and tropical design. The home of Sir Grantley Adams for 60 years, it is filled with his collection of antique furniture and memorabilia.

The chattel houses of the heritage village display the work of craftsmen and artists who work on-site. The houses are built of traditional materials and incorporate many carefully reproduced details, such as gingerbread trim, verandah latticework, and wooden shutters.

Stage One Theater Productions, established in 1979, concentrates on works about the Caribbean way of life. Its production of Errol John's *Moon on a Rainbow Shawl* has been a great success. In the play, the child Esther is talented in needlework and embroidery, but the patterns she creates are not those that her society encourages. She finds her own patterns "prettier, though much harder to do." The shawl she creates becomes a symbol of hope for all the aspects and identities of the Caribbean territories that have evolved from colonialism toward their independent future.

ARCHITECTURE

Architecture in Barbados is a blend of British tradition and tropical design, elegance, and simplicity. There are grand Georgian, Jacobean, and Victorian buildings on the one hand and basic wooden houses of the early settlers and slaves on the other. The wealth of the large sugar plantations resulted in the construction of great houses—solid structures built from natural coral limestone and furnished with mahogany furniture.

CHATTEL HOUSES

These simple, rectangular wooden homes—built on cement or stone blocks so that they could be moved—are often painted in combinations of vivid colors such as turquoise, lime, pink, and yellow. They are a favorite subject for culture-preserving painters such as Fielding Babb, Adrian Compton, the twin Stewart brothers, the twin Cumberbatch sisters, and Oscar Walkes.

Speightstown retains its early architecture. Bridgetown's colonial buildings on Broad Street exemplify the grandeur and architectural flourishes of the turn of the century, but they are now increasingly being surrounded by more modern structures. The public buildings with neo-Gothic facades, erected in the 19th century on the northern side of Trafalgar Square, accommodate the Houses of Parliament.

ARTS AND CRAFTS

It is difficult to distinguish between arts and crafts in Barbados. For centuries, artists and craftsmen have turned functional things into works of art by decorating everyday objects. Slaves did not have time to develop their art in traditional forms, so their art was often something practical rather than just decorative. This tradition survives today. For example, calabash pots, originally used to carry water, are often carved, decorated, and turned into handbags.

The Temple Yard Rastafarian community of craftsmen produces items made from leather, clay, wood, and straw. Akyem, who is a master of clay, produces plaques, low-relief scenes, and sculptures.

Karl Broodhagen has become perhaps the best-known sculptor and painter in Barbados. Many famous Barbadians, including Sir Grantley Adams, have been immortalized in bronze by him, but *The Emancipation Statue*, commemorating the 150th anniversary of emancipation, is perhaps his most outstanding work.

The island's chief showcase for handicrafts is Pelican Village near Bridgetown Harbor, which has galleries and workshops where craftsmen can display their products, including coconut-shell accessories, straw fans, bottle baskets, and mahogany objects such as key rings, jewelry boxes, ashtrays, coaster sets, and letter boxes. Pottery, wall hangings, woven baskets, mats, rugs, and shell and coral jewelry are also featured.

CHALKY MOUNT POTTERIES In the parish of Saint Andrew stands a hill of stratified clays of different colors—red, yellow, brown, and white—sandwiched between a thin strata of shale. For centuries this was the source of material for making household items such as lamps, candlestands, cups, plates, and bowls, as well as the clay pots used as stoves in many homes and the jugs called monkeys designed to cool beverages. The potter's craft has been handed down in families from generation to generation. Courtney Devonish, originally from Chalky Mount, has a gallery and workshop in Pelican Village. Trained in Italy, he is able to create classic European styles

Pottery on display at Chalky Mount.

as well as traditional island pottery.

ORNATE MURALS Local communities and schoolchildren are encouraged by the Cultural Foundation to create murals that depict cultural, historical, and social aspects of their neighborhoods as well as popular local characters. Such colorful representations of present-day Bajan daily life can be found on the walls of schools, community centers, and post offices.

LITERATURE

The island's high literacy rate has produced several respected novelists and poets who blended folk beliefs with their own experiences, creating a rich

REVELATION

H. A. Vaughan's Revelation, *dedicated to the black woman, is the most quoted poem to emerge from Barbados:*

Turn sideways now and let them see
What loveliness escapes the schools,
Then turn again, and smile, and be
The perfect answer to those fools
Who always prate of Greece and Rome
"The face that launched a thousand ships"
And such like things, but keep tight lips
For burnished beauty nearer home.
Turn in the sun, my love, my love!
What palmlike grace! What poise! I swear
I prize these dusky limbs above
My life. What laughing eyes! What gleaming hair!

literary tradition. In the 1940s the British Broadcasting Corporation radio program *Caribbean Voices* and the Barbadian magazine *Bim*, edited by Frank Collymore, brought to public notice writers such as George Lamming, Oliver Jackman, Derek Walcott, Monica Skeete, and others who later authored highly acclaimed novels and poetry.

Many early Bajan novels dealt with childhood, coming of age, and the search for self in a world of color and race, bondage, and freedom. George Lamming's *In the Castle of My Skin*, *The Emigrants*, and *Season of Adventure*, in which a mulatto woman searches for the meaning and value of her life when voodoo drums send her into a frenzy, have become classics. Geoffrey Drayton's *Christopher* deals with a white Bajan boy growing up in a black society, while Austin Clarke's *Amongst Thistles and Thorns* is the reverse—a black Bajan boy coming to terms with a white society.

Storytelling is the traditional way Bajans to entertain each other and pass on folk traditions. It has taken on an additional form today—local radio broadcasts of stories that focus on Barbadian culture and village life.

LEISURE

Locals and tourists alike take to the beautiful
waters of Barbados to unwind.

B

ARBADIANS AND VISITORS ALIKE find the island a perfect setting for a great variety of sports and other leisure activities.

Barbadians love to play, relax, and entertain themselves, and if they cannot afford the costly equipment required for some sports, they are happy to turn to pursuits that can be enjoyed inexpensively. The most popular sport in Barbados is cricket.

CRICKET

Cricket was introduced about 200 years ago by the British military, who regularly held cricket matches at the Garrison Savannah. It soon became

The West Indies cricket team during a test match held in Bridgetown.

The people of Barbados have a reputation for being avid sportsmen, and the island is known to provide world-class facilities and a broad range of activities on land and sea. Cricket, hiking, walking, running, dominoes, tennis, diving, surfing, windsurfing, snorkeling—all kinds of sports, recreation, and leisure pursuits are popular in Barbados.

popular with white planters and merchants, who set up their own clubs and organized matches. Cricket was considered to be character building and to reflect the nobler values of British culture.

In the early days the clubs such as the Wanderers (formed in 1877 by members of the mercantile community) and the Pickwick (formed by members of the plantocracy) were strictly white. Black and mixed-race professionals formed their own club, Spartan, whose members blackballed Herman Griffith, a public health inspector, because he was considered to be socially beneath them. Griffith's supporters broke away and formed the Empire Club, and Griffith became one of the great players of the game and the first black captain of a Barbados team. These four clubs are still active, but the structure of their membership has changed.

Early cricket was centered around Bridgetown and confined to a comparatively small portion of the population. Nevertheless, artisans and

Barbadians take up cricket at a young age. Many hope to play for the West Indies team, which selects its players from the best in the Caribbean.

other workers soon formed their own clubs. Recognizing the game's potential for building community spirit, plantation employers encouraged their workers to play cricket by providing them with land for a pitch and supplying them with secondhand equipment no longer needed by their own clubs. These teams arranged their own competitions, and rivalry was intense.

When the Barbados Cricket League was formed, it brought the different groups of cricketers together. The white plantation owners and business executives found camaraderie with and respect for the black civil servants and lawyers they played against. Cricket can thus be said to have helped pave the way to independence.

When Barbados became independent in 1966, it challenged the rest of the world to a showcase cricket match. It remains one of the international capitals of cricket and always contributes a large contingent to the West Indies team.

Test cricket is played at international levels between January and April in Kensington Oval, which is filled to its 15,000-spectator capacity. The Cricket Association and the Cricket League have matches on Saturday afternoons and sometimes on Sundays during a season lasting from early June to mid-September.

Friendly matches are played on beaches, open pastures, and village fields year-round. Young boys who dream of escaping from poverty and making a name for themselves know that mastering cricket could mean more to their future than any other skill. As a result, they play cricket anywhere, anytime.

Bridgetown-born Garfield Sobers is acknowledged to be one of the world's greatest cricket players. He represented the West Indies 93 times.

OTHER SPORTS

SOFTBALL Using tennis balls and slim mahogany bats instead of instead of leather balls and regulation willow bats from England, this modified form of cricket is played on Sunday mornings, when more than 100 softball teams compete for places on the Barbados teams that regularly tour the United States and Canada.

RUNNING Long-distance running is a popular activity in Barbados. All over the island, men and women walking briskly or jogging have become a common sight. An annual Run Barbados International Road Race is held on the first weekend in December. The 26-mile (42-km) marathon over paved roads along the coast and in and around Bridgetown attracts male and female competitors from around the world.

The Garrison Savannah in Bridgetown is a popular place for joggers.

Scuba divers off Saint James. Most beach resorts have facilities that cater to water sports.

DOMINOES This game, played with such enthusiasm that the slap of the dominoes on the table can be startling, is the national table game. Every June the world's top dominoes players come to compete in the World Dominoes Festival.

GOLF Five golf courses and fine weather year-round help make Barbados a popular golfing destination. The versatile cricket legend Sir Garfield Sobers has also captained the Barbados golf team.

WATER SPORTS Constant sunshine and steady breezes on the southern coast produce ideal conditions for windsurfing. At the Soup Bowl, a bay near Bathsheba, waves from the Atlantic Ocean and clean, shark-free waters create equally ideal conditions for surfers.

Yachting is another popular sport. Coral reefs and sunken wrecks in clear water surrounding the island also provide scuba-diving enthusiasts with excellent diving sites.

Farley Hill National Park.

NATIONAL PARKS

Several national parks on the island have become popular recreation areas for both Barbadians and visitors. Perhaps the best known, Farley Hill National Park consists of several acres of tropical trees and plants on a cliff up to 899 feet (274 m) above sea level, overlooking the Scotland District. Bought by the Barbados government and declared a national park, it was officially opened by Queen Elizabeth II on February 15, 1966, just several months before the island's independence.

The original mansion in the park was built on the grand scale of 19th-century plantation houses. After the owner, Thomas Graham Briggs, died in 1887, the mansion lost its elegance. Even so, Hollywood moviemakers chose it for the Fleury home, Belfontaine, in the movie of Alec Waugh's novel *Island in the Sun*. In 1956 the crumbling old palace was transformed at enormous cost into a mansion worthy of a sugar baron. A new gallery and stairway were built, and an open verandah was added in front of the main entrance, where an artificial lake was constructed. Unfortunately a few years later a great fire destroyed everything except the walls.

RUM SHOPS

Gatherings of family and friends for Sunday lunches are a favorite weekend activity. Even more popular with men, however, are get-togethers on Sunday mornings at the island's numerous rum shops to discuss topics ranging from politics to cricket.

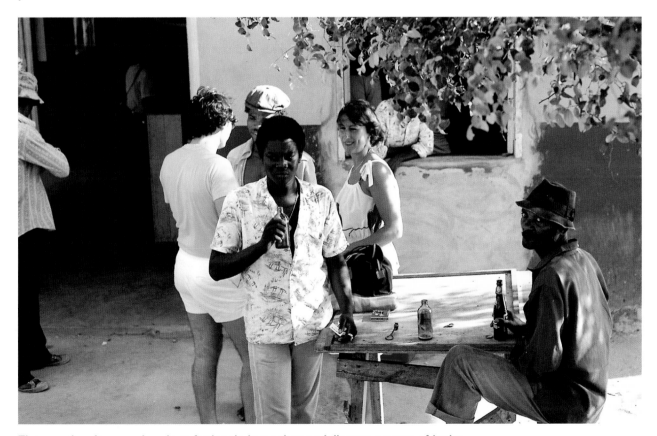

The rum shop is a popular place for locals to meet up and discuss a range of topics.

FESTIVALS

A girl dressed in a costume for the
Crop Over Festival parade.

BESIDES RELIGIOUS HOLIDAYS SUCH as Easter and Christmas, Barbadians look forward to six major events in the festive calendar every year.

These are the Jazz Festival (held in January), the Holetown Festival (from February 17), the Oistins Fish Festival (Easter weekend), the De Congaline Carnival (from April 23), the Crop Over Festival (from mid-June), and the National Independence Festival of Creative Arts (throughout November).

A number of sports festivals, such as the Mount Gay International Regatta (January), the Mountain Bike Festival (February), the

A man dressed in a vibrant costume for a parade.

Barbados enjoys a variety of festivals throughout the year, from carnivals to street fairs, from culinary feasts to sports celebrations to cultural events. The combination of British, African, American, and Amerindian elements ensures that the festivals are an exhilarating, colorful, and dramatic demonstration of the living culture of the Bajan people.

International Netball Clubs Festival (June), and the Banks Hockey Festival (August), as well as several cricket festivals, are also held throughout the year.

JAZZ FESTIVAL

In January top-class performers from all over the world come to Barbados to provide a weekend of the best jazz talents against a backdrop of tropical splendor.

HOLETOWN FESTIVAL

The site of the landing of the first permanent settlers on February 17, 1627, is the setting for

Young Barbadians take a break from the festivities of the Holetown Festival.

a week of continuous entertainment each year. Medieval songs are sung in churches, whereas more modern beats can be heard in the fairgrounds. Jazz, gospel, brass, and folk concerts are held by the light of the moon on the beach where the first 80 settlers landed nearly 400 years ago.

OISTINS FISH FESTIVAL

Held over the Easter weekend, this festival pays tribute to the island's fishing folk, who hold competitions over several days to demonstrate their skills in fishing, fish deboning, boat racing, and even crab racing. Spectators throng the beaches, marketplaces, and rum shops that line the roadsides and dance to steel bands.

DE CONGALINE CARNIVAL

Ten days of festivities begin on April 23, climaxing on May 1 with the massive May Day parade, when thousands dance to hot calypso rhythms. Live musical

The grand finale of Crop Over, Kadooment Day, is marked by a carnival parade.

performances run during the days in between. Barbados's only steel-band competition is one of the major attractions. The De Congaline Festival has been celebrated since the early 1990s.

CROP OVER FESTIVAL

The origins of the Crop Over Festival can be traced back to the 1780s, when plantation managers used to hold a "dinner and sober dance" to celebrate harvest time, or Crop Over. Before emancipation, planters had to support their slaves year-round, but after 1838, Crop Over meant both less work and lower wages for many workers. For a final end-of-harvest celebration, farmworkers would use refuse from sugarcane plants to create a stuffed figure of a man they called Mr. Harding, who symbolized the period of time between sugar crops, when employment and money were scarce. Workers would parade around the plantation yards in their carts, their animals decorated with flamboyant frangipani and other flowers, and introduce Mr. Harding to the plantation manager. Then they would adjourn for dancing and food, with salted meat and rum contributed by the manager.

As the sugar industry in Barbados declined so too did the Crop Over Festival, and in the 1940s the festival was abandoned completely. It was revived in 1974, however, to pay tribute to the vital role of sugar in Barbados's history, and other elements of Barbadian culture were introduced to make the festival that exists today. Perhaps the most elaborate and important festival in the country, Crop Over lasts for five weeks, from mid-June to August. The Ceremonial Delivery of the Last Canes opens the festivities and

Costume designers compete for the coveted best designer award in the Kadooment Day carnival parade.

BARBADOS'S PUBLIC HOLIDAYS

New Year's Day	January 1
Errol Barrow Day	January 21
Good Friday and Easter Monday	late March/early April
May Day	May 1
Whit Monday	eighth Monday after Easter
Kadooment Day	first Monday in August
United Nations Day	first Monday in October
Independence Day	November 30
Christmas Day	December 25
Boxing Day	December 26

is followed over the next few weeks by attractions such as a decorated cart parade and a calypso competition.

The Cohobblopot variety show, which blends drama, dance, and music with the crowning of the king and queen of the costumed bands, is another major draw. The massive Bridgetown Market street fair offers selections of Bajan cooking and local arts and crafts. The king of calypso is crowned at the Pic-o-de-Crop Show. The climax of the festival is Kadooment Day on the first Monday in August, which is a national holiday. Revelers dress up in spectacular costumes and dance along the streets in a huge carnival parade to the most popular calypso and soca sounds. At the end of the route, a lively fete takes place with more music, color, fun, and food.

NATIONAL INDEPENDENCE FESTIVAL OF CREATIVE ARTS

Bajans of all ages match their talents in music, singing, dancing, acting, and writing during the festival. Performances by the finalists are held on Independence Day, November 30.

FOOD

A street vendor selling fruit.

BARBADOS OFFERS AN ENORMOUS variety of gastronomic delights, including spicy Bajan and other Caribbean specialties. Some of these dishes borrow heavily from African, Indian, and even Chinese sources.

TRADITIONAL FOODS

***COU-COU* AND SALT FISH**   African inspired, *cou-cou* (koo-koo) is considered the Bajan national dish. A mixture of cornmeal and okra is

Bustling crowds at the Friday Market at Oistins.

A flying-fish burger.

stirred vigorously to prevent lumps, packed into a bowl, and then turned out onto a plate. A depression is made in the center, and a sauce is ladled into this and around the mound. *Cou-cou* is traditionally served with salt fish. Originally imported to feed the slaves because it was an inexpensive source of protein, salt fish is now regarded as a delicacy.

FLYING FISH AND OTHER SEAFOOD Virtually a national symbol, flying fish is perhaps the most popular Bajan delicacy. Caught between December and June, it is frozen or dried for use during the rest of the year. It can be prepared in many ways, from beachside sandwiches (called fish cutters) to gourmet dishes. Fresh from the surrounding waters come other seafood, such as lobster, shrimp, dorado, turtle, red snapper, tuna, kingfish, and mackerel. Unique are the crane chubb and sea eggs (white sea urchins' roe, which are deviled, breaded, or prepared to taste).

STEW FOOD Barbadians love pork, and every bit of the pig is used in some way or another. Traditionally cooked midweek when fresh or more-expensive foods run out, stew food is made from finely chopped pig's tail, snout, head, and trotters. It is cooked with green vegetables, such as okra, squash, cabbage, or spinach, and served with ground provisions—root vegetables such as yams, sweet potatoes, and cassava—as well as breadfruit.

PUDDING AND SOUSE Pudding, which resembles a long dark sausage, is made from grated, well-seasoned sweet potato stuffed into a cleaned pig's intestine and steamed. The sausage is then cut into slices and served with souse made from pork—including the head and the trotters—cooked, sliced, and soused (pickled) with lime juice, onion, hot pepper, salt, chopped cucumber, and parsley. This dish is a traditional Saturday night meal for family get-togethers. Leftovers are usually fried and served for breakfast the following day.

FRUITS AND VEGETABLES

Barbados's tropical climate yields fruits such as mangoes, papayas, bananas, guavas, avocados, and coconuts in abundance. Other fruits eaten include Barbados cherries and soursops—large green fruits with a slightly acidic, pulpy texture that are often made into a refreshing drink. Breadfruit is a staple in the Bajan diet. The size of a melon, breadfruit has white starchy and slightly spongy flesh that can be cooked in stews, fried, boiled, or pickled.

Breadfruit growing on a tree.

Also abundant are vegetables and fruits such as yams, eggplants, okras, pumpkins, plantains (resembling large bananas, these starchy fruits are usually fried or grilled and eaten as a accompaniment to other dishes), squashes, and christophenes, a common Caribbean vegetable shaped like a large pear that can be eaten raw in salads, used in soups, or cooked like squash.

OTHER BAJAN SPECIALTIES

Some other popular Bajan dishes include:

- *jug-jug* (jugg-jugg), a mixture of Guinea corn, green peas, and salted meat.
- pepperpot, a spicy stew made with a variety of meats.
- *roti* (ROW-tee), a curry filling of meat or chicken and potatoes wrapped in a tortillalike flatbread.

A boy enjoys a simple meal.

- *conkies* (kon-kees), a mixture of cornmeal, coconut, pumpkin, raisins, sweet potatoes, and spices, steamed in a plantain leaf.

SUNDAY BUFFETS

The Bajan custom of entertaining family and friends on the weekend is still popular, and Sunday buffets in particular provide a good excuse for festive parties with plentiful food, drink, and music.

STREET THAT NEVER SLEEPS

In Bridgetown, Baxter Road becomes a party every night when rum shops and restaurants open their doors, and music and wonderful aromas fill the air. At one end, vendors stand over buckpots, or old cast-iron pots, deep-frying fish, chicken, or pork Bajan-style over bright coal fires. Locals and visitors mingle, eating and drinking until the early hours of the morning.

FISH FRY

The coastal town of Oistins is considered the place to be on Friday and Saturday nights, in part because of its famous Fish Fry. This is a market on the beach where freshly caught fish and other seafood are cooked according to local recipes. There are numerous vendors to choose from, and music fills the air, making for a memorable evening out. Bajans and visitors eat their fill and dance the night away.

HAWKERS AND HUCKSTERS

Hawkers sell fresh produce, sometimes from a small van, or the back of a bicycle, or just a regular spot on a street corner. They usually sell Wednesdays to Saturdays and spend Monday or Tuesday obtaining their particular produce from farms or plantations, often harvesting it themselves. Hawking is most profitable in the largest towns, where there is passing trade, so hawkers are found mostly in Bridgetown, Oistins, and Speightstown.

Hucksters sell candy, chips, corn curls, and popcorn outside schools and at events or festivals. Sometimes they bake and sell traditional peanut cakes or chocolate fudge. These are normally sold out of cabinets to protect them from flies.

DRINKS

RUM Rum is the social drink of Barbados. It is drunk at weddings, births, christenings, wakes, and funerals, as well as on any other occasion that is a reason for celebrating. It may be drunk straight from a bottle passed from hand to hand, with ice, or diluted with fruit juices in the form of delicious rum punches.

When it was first made in the 1640s, by distilling the juice extracted from molasses (the thick liquid residue left after most of the sugar has been taken out of the sugarcane juice), rum was not as refined as it is today. Then, it was called rumbullion because it was so potent. Planters sold their rum to ships

A man drinking rum punch.

for consumption by the crews and resale overseas and to the taverns that sprang up all over the island and later became rum shops. Rum was in great demand and helped to make the planters prosperous.

There are nearly 1,000 rum shops on the island today. They have become much more than shops selling rum. Functioning more like village stores selling groceries and fuel, they are informal community centers where men meet to exchange "gup and gossip," discuss politics, or simply hang out. Women rarely frequent rum shops and then only with a male escort.

Among internationally recognized brands, Mount Gay Rum claims to be the oldest in the Caribbean, and possibly all over the world. A legal document dated February 29, 1703, lists "two stone windmills, one boiling house with seven coppers, one curing house, and one still house"—all equipment essential for the making of rum—on the Mount Gilboa plantation. John Sober had inherited Mount Gilboa from his father, William Sandiford, in 1747. As an absentee landlord he appointed his friend, Sir John Gay Alleyne, to manage the estate on his behalf. The estate became hugely successful and was renamed Mount Gay to honor Sir John Gay Alleyne after he died in 1801.

High-quality sugarcane and crystal-clear water are the basic ingredients for making rum. Single and double distillations of the spirit are produced and stored in charred-oak barrels that are left to age in cellars for various lengths of time, eventually to be married (blended) by a master blender in accordance with secret recipes.

BEER AND OTHER DRINKS The island beer, Banks, is popular with both locals and visitors. Other popular drinks include coconut water, fresh lemonade, and punches made from the juices of fruits such as mangoes, guavas, soursops, passion fruits, and tamarinds.

Mauby (maw-bee) is made by boiling bits of the bitter bark of the soldierwood (*Colubrina elliptica*) with spices. It is then strained and sweetened. Sorrel, the local Christmas drink, is prepared from the fresh or dried red sepals of the sorrel plant, which are boiled or infused in hot water with spices and rum added. *Falernum* (fal-er-nerm) is a local liqueur made with lime juice, granulated sugar, rum, and water that has been flavored with almond extract.

BARBADOS PORK ROAST

This is a popular Sunday favorite and should be served with boiled or steamed fresh vegetables.

3 pounds (1.4 kg) boneless pork loin roast
½ teaspoon (2.5 ml) salt
1 tablespoon (15 ml) ground cumin
1 teaspoon (5 ml) brown sugar
1 teaspoon (5 ml) ground cinnamon
1 tablespoon (15 ml) chili powder
1½ teaspoons (7 ml) ground coriander
1½ teaspoons (7 ml)ground black pepper
1 teaspoon (5 ml) cayenne pepper

Preheat oven to 350°F (180°C). Dry the surface of the pork with a paper towel. Mix together the remaining ingredients and then rub the mixture all over the pork. Place the pork in a roasting pan and put it in the oven. Cook for about one hour. Remove from oven, and let the meat rest for about 10 minutes. Slice and serve.

COCONUT SUGAR CAKES

This is a favorite Bajan recipe for everyone with a sweet tooth!

¾ pound (350 g) sugar
¼ pint (156 ml) water
½ pound (227 g) grated fresh coconut

Put the sugar in a saucepan and add the water. Simmer until the sugar has melted, and then add the coconut. Boil the mixture slowly, stirring to avoid burning. Cook until the mixture has thickened and takes on a greasy look. Drop the mixture by teaspoonfuls onto a cookie sheet that has been moistened with water. Leave to cool and set.

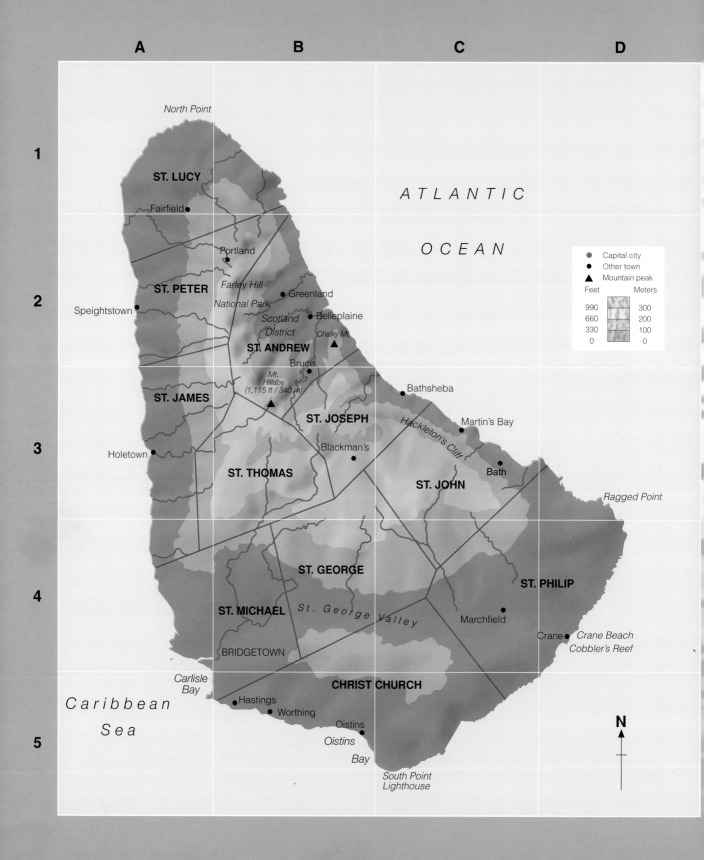

A   B   C   D

1

North Point

ST. LUCY

Fairfield●

Portland●

ST. PETER

Farley Hill

2

Speightstown●

National Park

●Greenland

Scotland
District

●Belleplaine

Chalky Mt. ▲

ST. ANDREW

Bruce●

Mt.
Hillaby
(1,115 ft / 340 m) ▲

ST. JAMES

ST. JOSEPH

●Bathsheba

Martin's Bay●

Hackleton's Cliff

Blackman's●

3

Holetown●

ST. THOMAS

ST. JOHN

Bath●

Ragged Point

4

ST. GEORGE

ST. PHILIP

ST. MICHAEL

St. George Valley

Marchfield●

BRIDGETOWN

Crane● *Crane Beach*
Cobbler's Reef

Carlisle
Bay

CHRIST CHURCH

Caribbean
Sea

Hastings●
●Worthing

Oistins●

Oistins

5

Bay

South Point
Lighthouse

ATLANTIC

OCEAN

● Capital city
● Other town
▲ Mountain peak

Feet   Meters

990   300
660   200
330   100
0   0

N

MAP OF BARBADOS

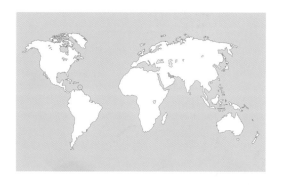

ECONOMIC BARBADOS

Services
 Airport

Port

Agriculture
Fishing

Fish processing

Sugar processing

Natural Resources
Oil fields

Manufacturing
Cement

Pottery

Rum

ABOUT THE ECONOMY

OVERVIEW

Throughout history, the Barbadian economy was based on sugarcane cultivation and related activities. Tourism has become the most important industry and the main revenue earner for Barbados. Informatics and offshore financing are also major foreign-exchange earners, with Barbados benefiting from a highly educated workforce and having the same time zone as the financial centers of the eastern United States. Since 2003, growth has picked up, boosted by an increase in tourism and construction. As a result of preparations made to host the Cricket World Cup in 2007, there was an increase in transportation, communications, construction, and utilities spending, but the sector experienced declines in revenue with the global economic downturn of 2008 to 2009. Barbados became a member of CARICOM in 1973.

GROSS DOMESTIC PRODUCT (GDP)

$5.466 billion (2008 estimate)

CURRENCY

The Barbados dollar
1 dollar = 100 cents
US$1 = Bds$2

GDP PER CAPITA

$19,300 (2008 estimate)

GROWTH RATE

1.5 percent (2008 estimate)

MAIN EXPORTS

Sugar and molasses, rum, foodstuffs, beer, chemicals, electronic/electrical components, clothing

MAIN IMPORTS

Consumer goods, machinery, foodstuffs, construction materials, chemicals, automobiles, fuel

LABOR FORCE

142,000 (2006 estimate)

TOURISM

567,667 visitors (2008 estimate)

MAIN TRADE PARTNERS

United States, Trinidad and Tobago, United Kingdom, Saint Lucia, Jamaica, Saint Vincent

AGRICULTURAL PRODUCTS

Sugar, hops, vegetables, cotton

NATURAL RESOURCES

Oil, natural gas

CULTURAL BARBADOS

ANIMAL FLOWER CAVE
An amazing cave that opens into the sea. The name is derived from the sea anemones living in the pools in the cave.

SAINT NICHOLAS ABBEY
Built in 1660, this is one of the three genuine Jacobean mansions in the Western Hemisphere.

HARRISON'S CAVE
Crystallized limestone cavern and a marvel of stalagmites, stalactites, waterfalls, and deep emerald pools.

TYROL COT
Constructed in 1854, the one-time home of Sir Grantley Adams, the first premier of Barbados, has been restored by the Barbados National Trust. A heritage village surrounds the house and is a "living museum" with arts and crafts being sold from chattel houses.

BANKS BREWERY
Barbados beer brewing and bottling plant.

MOUNT GAY RUM VISITORS CENTER
Discover the colorful history of Mount Gay Rum and see how the local rum is produced.

GEORGE WASHINGTON HOUSE
George Washington visited the island in 1751 and stayed at this location. It was Washington's only trip outside the United States.

SAM LORD'S CASTLE
Sam Lord's Castle is a Georgian mansion built in 1820 by the buccaneer Samuel Hall Lord. Legend has it that Sam Lord acquired his wealth by plundering ships that he lured onto reefs off the coast by hanging lanterns in coconut trees.

MORGAN LEWIS MILL
Maintained by the Barbados National Trust, Morgan Lewis Mill is one of only two intact and restored sugar mills in the Caribbean. The mill includes an exhibit of the equipment used to produce sugar when the industry was run by wind power.

GRENADE HALL FOREST AND SIGNAL STATION
Historic signal station and forest.

BATHSHEBA
Fishing village, park, and picnic area with a dramatic rugged coastal landscape and striking rock formations. A popular surfing spot, the waters have a strong undertow.

ANDROMEDA BOTANICAL GARDENS
Six acres (2.5 ha) of gardens with more than 600 species of plants including orchids, hibiscuses, palms, and cacti.

SUNBURY PLANTATION HOUSE
Built around 1600 by Matthew Chapman, an English planter and one of the first settlers on the island, this heritage house is a living monument to plantation life of a bygone era and has been carefully restored.

SOUTH POINT LIGHTHOUSE
Assembled in 1852, this was the first lighthouse on the island. It was refurbished and repainted in 2004.

ABOUT THE CULTURE

OFFICIAL NAME
Barbados

CAPITAL
Bridgetown

AREA
166 square miles (431 square km)

POPULATION
284,589 (2009 estimate)

PARISHES
Barbados is divided into 11 administrative parishes: Christ Church, Saint Andrew, Saint George, Saint James, Saint John, Saint Joseph, Saint Lucy, Saint Michael, Saint Peter, Saint Philip, Saint Thomas

MAJOR CITIES
Bridgetown, Speightstown, Oistins, Holetown

OFFICIAL LANGUAGE
English

MAJOR RELIGIONS
Protestant, 63.4 percent (Anglican, 28.3 percent; Pentecostal, 18.7 percent; Methodist, 5.1 percent; others, 11.3 percent); Roman Catholic, 4.2 percent; other Christian, 7 percent; other, 4.8 percent; none or unspecified, 20.6 percent (2008 estimate)

BIRTHRATE
12.48 births per 1,000 population (2008 estimate)

DEATH RATE
8.58 deaths per 1,000 population (2008 estimate)

INFANT MORTALITY RATE
11.05 deaths per 1,000 live births

FERTILITY RATE
1.65 children born per woman

LIFE EXPECTANCY
Total population 73.21 years
Male: 71.2 years
Female: 75.24 years (2008 estimate)

MAIN POLITICAL PARTIES
Barbados Labor Party (BLP)
Democratic Labor Party (DLP)
National Democratic Party (NDP)

PROMINENT BARBADIANS
Sir Garfield Sobers, the Mighty Gabby, Frank Collymore

ANNIVERSARIES
Errol Barrow Day (January 21)
Independence Day (November 30)

TIME LINE

IN BARBADOS	IN THE WORLD

1623 B.C.
First settlement at Port Saint Charles

116–17 B.C.
The Roman Empire reach its greatest extent, under Emperor Trajan (98–17).

A.D. 500
The Barrancoid Indians arrive from Trinidad, but by A.D. 600 there is no record of them in Barbados.

800
The Arawak Indians arrive in Barbados.

1200
The Carib Indians conquer the Arawak Indians; the Carib Indians disappear by 1500.

1206–1368
Genghis Khan unifies the Mongols and starts conquest of the world. At its height, the Mongol Empire under Kublai Khan stretches from China to Persia and parts of Europe and Russia.

1530
Beginning of transatlantic slave trade organized by the Portuguese in Africa.

1625
Captain John Powell lands on Barbados and claims the island for King James I of England.

1627
English settlers establish a colony and develop sugar plantations using slaves brought from Africa.

1663
Barbados is made an English crown possession.

1789–99
The French Revolution

1816
A black slave named Bussa leads a slave revolt and is subsequently executed.

1834
Slavery is abolished.

1914
World War I begins.

1937
Riots break out because of poor economic conditions; British Royal Commission is sent to investigate; Grantley Adams establishes the Barbados Labor Party (BLP).

1939
World War II begins.

1945
The United States drops atomic bombs on Hiroshima and Nagasaki. World War II ends.

IN BARBADOS	IN THE WORLD
1951	
Universal adult suffrage is introduced, and the BLP wins general elections.	
1954	
Ministerial government is set up with Grantley Adams as premier.	
1955	
Democratic Labor Party (DLP) is formed.	
1958	
Barbados becomes a member of British-sponsored Federation of the West Indies.	
1961	
Barbados gains full internal self-government.	
1966	**1966**
Barbados becomes independent.	The Chinese Cultural Revolution
1967	
Barbados joins the United Nations.	
1983	**1986**
Barbados supports and provides a base for the U.S. invasion of Grenada.	Nuclear power disaster at Chernobyl in Ukraine
	1991
	Breakup of the Soviet Union
	1997
	Hong Kong is returned to China.
1999	**2001**
The BLP wins a landslide election, with 26 of 28 seats in the House of Assembly.	Terrorists crash planes into New York, Washington D.C., and Pennsylvania.
2003	
The BLP wins general elections; Owen Arthur returns for a third term.	
2004	
Sea border disagreement with Trinidad and Tobago; Barbados takes its case to a UN-backed tribunal.	
2008	**2008**
Parliamentary elections won by opposition DLP; David Thompson becomes prime minister.	Earthquake in Sichuan Province, China, kills thousands.

GLOSSARY

Arawaks
Early inhabitants of Barbados, who originally came from South America.

baccoo (bah-KOO)
Tiny spirit believed to bestow good or evil, depending on the amount of attention he receives.

Bajan
The word *Bajan* is a contraction of the word *Barbadian*. It is a term used to describe the people of Barbados, or Barbadians, as well as the spoken and written dialect, which uses a mixture of British English and West African syntax.

Caribs
An aggressive tribe who settled in the Caribbean islands, including Barbados, displacing the Arawaks.

casareep (ka-sa-REEP)
An original Arawak flavoring made from grated, ground cassava still used in cooking today.

chattel houses
Movable dwellings.

conkies (kon-kees).
A mixture of cornmeal, coconut, pumpkin, raisins, sweet potatoes, and spices, steamed in a plantain leaf.

conrad (KON-rad)
Avenging ghost.

duppy (DOO-pee)
Spirit of the dead who roams at night.

duppy dust
Grave dirt or pulverized human bones that are believed to have the power to kill if thrown on a victim.

hags
Ugly spirits, usually of planters' wives, who shed their skin and traveled about as balls of fire.

high whites
Descendants of the elite planter families who still control much of Barbados's commercial life.

jug-jug (jugg-jugg)
Dish of corn, green peas, and salted meat.

obeah
A form of witchcraft.

parish
Unit of local administration.

plantocracy
Wealthy planter class.

red legs
Descendants of white indentured servants.

soca
A form of dance music with bold rhythms and heavy bass sounds frequently played during carnivals.

FOR FURTHER INFORMATION

BOOKS

Harrington, Sean. *The A to Z of Barbados Heritage*. Oxford, England: Macmillan Caribbean, 2004.

Laurie, Peter and Toy, Mike. *Barbados: An Island Portrait*. Oxford, England: Macmillan Caribbean, 2005.

Menard, R. R. *Sugar, Slavery, and Plantation Agriculture in Early Barbados*. Charlottesville, VA: University of Virginia Press, 2006.

Orr, Tamra B. *Barbados* (Discovering the Caribbean). Broomall, PA: Mason Crest Publishers, 2003.

Pariser, Harr S. *Explore Barbados*. San Francisco: Manatee Press, 2009.

FILMS

Chattel House. Gladstone Yearwood, 2004.

Island in the Sun. 1957 film starring Harry Belafonte. Irving Burgie wrote two songs for the film: "Lead Man Holler" and the title song. It was filmed partially in Barbados.

MUSIC

King, John and various artists. *Soundtrip Barbados*. Reise-Know-How Sound GmbH & Co., 2009.

Kirton, David. *Time for Change*. Phantom Sound & Vision, 2008.

Manning, Marvo, Alfred Pagnell, and Andrea Gollop. *Dumplings in de Stew*, 2004.

Rihanna. *Music of the Sun*. Mercury Records, 2005.

BIBLIOGRAPHY

BOOKS

Beckles, Hilary. *A History of Barbados*. Cambridge, England: Cambridge University Press, 1990.

Broberg, Merle. *Places and Peoples of the World: Barbados.* New York: Chelsea House, 1989.

Forde, G. Addington, Sean Carrington, Henry Fraser, and John Gilmore. *The A to Z of Barbadian Heritage.* Bridgetown, Barbados: Heinemann Caribbean, 1990.

Handler, Jerome S. *Plantation Slavery in Barbados*. Cambridge, MA: Harvard University Press, 1978.

Lamming, George. *In the Castle of My Skin*. London: Schocken, 1983.

Puckrein, G. A. *Little England: Plantation Society and Anglo-Barbadian Politics 1627–1700.* New York: New York University Press, 1984.

WEBSITES

Barbados Government Information Service. www.barbados.gov.bb/bgis.htm

BBC Country Profile: Barbados. http://news.bbc.co.uk/2/hi/americas/country_profiles/1154116.stm

CIA World Factbook. www.cia.gov/index.html

Encyclopaedia Britannica. www.britannica.com/

Fact Monster. www.factmonster.com/

Infoplease. www.infoplease.com/

Irving Burgie. www.irvingburgie.com/barbados/slideshow/barbados_bio.swf

Totally Barbados. www.totallybarbados.com/

United Nations Environment Programme. www.unep.org/

INDEX

INDEX